This Business of Therapy

A Practical Guide
To Starting, Developing And Sustaining A Therapy
Practice

Jude Fay

Preface By Ger Murphy

Published By This Business Of Therapy & Jude Fay
Naas, Co Kildare

Get my free report "Five Ways To Boost Your Therapy Practice" from my website www.thisbusinessoftherapy.com or http://tinyurl.com/h3xv49r

Published by This Business of Therapy & Jude Fay, November 2016

Dedication

Dedicated to my mother, Reine, my husband, Peter, and my children, Simon and Rosie.

My greatest teachers.

Preface

It gives me great pleasure to offer a preface to Jude's new book. Firstly, I want to say that I warmly endorse the book. I think it is a much-needed book in relation to psychotherapy and counselling in Ireland, as this is the first book dealing with the issue of business practice in the field.

It is also a challenging book. Most psychotherapists are more comfortable reading of issues of the inner world and may turn away from a book on business practice, but we are running businesses, and if we saw such avoidant behaviour in our clients we might wonder with them how this served them, and so we may want to challenge ourselves to consider these issues.

The development of a business is often a subject far from the forefront of the minds of counsellors and psychotherapists when they are undertaking their training. In running psychotherapy and counselling training for over 20 years at the Institute of Creative Counselling and Psychotherapy, I found that the perceived need for and interest in looking at issues of practice and business development slowly grew from the late 1980s to 2010 as the profession grew substantially and thereby business competition grew accordingly. Trainees and therapists can have a negative attitude to business and to the basic issue of making a good living from the work, as if to do so was to sully the work in some way. Right now, feel for a moment your internal response if I say that we are going to have a business conversation as against a spiritual one. How is your internal response different and what might this tell you?

Like all humans, we can split the world into the areas where we are comfortable and those where we are not, and we stay where we are comfortable. We can feel that we will not be proficient outside our area of comfort, and can have a magical viewpoint that the work will come if it is meant to, etc. Yet we know from our therapeutic work and from ecology that growth and change happens most at the edges, the transitional spaces, the boundaries. So I invite us to take the journey clearly mapped out here by Jude, and see how we may benefit, and how our practices may be stronger.

I believe that the value of this book is not only for the benefit of the individual practitioner, but also has a wider benefit. A strong majority of the profession are female, often a second earner in a family, or being supported by pensions or past income. This has had the effect of keeping many men who might see themselves as the primary earner in a family away from a career in psychotherapy or counselling. In these times where psychological difficulties in males are rampant, with a significantly higher number of young men killing themselves and the rate of young male self-inflicted death being fourth highest in the EU, there is a great need for young and older male clients having a real choice of therapists of both genders. This book may be a step in strengthening the business aspect of therapy and thus bringing a broader cross-section of practitioners into the profession.

I have great pleasure in recommending this book to you.

Ger Murphy,

M.I.A.H.I.P

Director, Institute of Creative Counselling and Psychotherapy Dublin

Former Chair of IAHIP and Irish Council Of Psychotherapy

TABLE OF CONTENTS

Part 1:

Let's Get Started

Introduction

Congratulations. You've made the decision to go into practice as a counsellor or therapist. It's a big decision and I wish you well with it. May you attract the work you desire and grow and prosper in your career. Moreover, may you see your clients heal and grow.

I hope you will find this book useful in setting up or developing your practice. I have tried to make it practical and straightforward. While you may not always agree with my point of view, I hope that I will provide you with food for thought. Inevitably, there will be issues that you encounter that I have not addressed here. I'd love to hear from you, and I'd be happy to help you with those challenges if I can. You can contact me at jude.fay@thisbusinessoftherapy.com

Why I Wrote This Book

I trained many years ago as a Chartered Accountant and worked in that profession for many years. I was a partner in a three-partner practice for some of that time, and for a short stretch, practised as a sole practitioner. I also worked for the governing body for chartered accountants as a consultant to practitioners starting up and running their own practices. So when it came to setting up as a therapist, I had no doubts that I had all the experience, skills and know-how to make the business side of it work.

Was I wrong? Not wrong, perhaps, but definitely a little naïve.

I forgot to take into account two very important factors:

1. Working for or with an established organisation is very different from working on your own, and

2. When I practised as an accountant, I wasn't feeling much!!

So when I first started up in my own therapy practice, some of what I thought should have been easy for me, given my background, was surprisingly difficult. The absence of a monthly or weekly salary left me feeling insecure, vulnerable and desperate to attract paying clients. Finishing my training and launching myself into the "real world" found me grieving for the guidance of my tutors and the fellowship of other students. And the absence of a surrounding organisation to give me structure and momentum at that time left me struggling with procrastination and indecision.

I was blessed to have the support of my good friend, Jennifer, as we established ourselves together, sharing tasks and roles, and egging each other on. To be honest, I doubt I would have made it on my own.

I feel very strongly that it really shouldn't be that hard. So I started "This Business of Therapy." It was a very gradual process, starting with chatting with some friends about how we'd gone about setting up our practices, sharing the experiences of what worked and what didn't. I did the odd workshop and wrote an occasional article, and slowly began to realise that I could help to make it a bit easier for others by sharing what I know. So here I am, writing to you, hoping that something I say in these pages will make your journey a little easier!

How To Get The Most From This Book

This is a long book, and there are many ideas and suggestions included in here. You don't have to implement them all. Take your time, take it slowly; you have the whole of your practising life ahead of you. Some of what is here will fit for you, and some will not. I have tried to cover as many angles as I can, so feel free to pick and choose what's relevant and what's not. If something I say doesn't feel right for you, perhaps it will prompt you to a strategy or solution that works better. Focus on one small piece at a time, as in that way you're less likely to get overwhelmed and throw it to one side.

The book largely presumes that you will be self-employed, and as such making all the decisions about what you and your practice need. However, you may still find a lot to think about if you decide to work for or with someone else.

Expectations

Your training process has probably taken some years. Maybe you have changed career, or are coming back to work after an absence, or perhaps you have been employed and are now embarking on self-employment. Whatever your journey to get to this place, you will be eager to start the process. You probably have expectations about how it will be for you. Are you feeling excitement at this new venture? Do you have doubts or fears? You may be impatient to get started, to realise your vision, or you may be hesitant. Whatever you're feeling, take a moment to acknowledge that this is the beginning, hopefully of a rewarding and satisfying process that will bring growth, learning and prosperity to you and those you work with.

The average small business, whatever its nature –a grocery shop, a hairdresser, or a professional practice – takes at least two to three years to get up and running. So don't expect everything to come together on day one. There is both an emotional and a practical journey to go through, and they each take their time. A seed takes time to grow into a tree, and it will take time for the idea of starting your own practice to grow from initial conception into the reality of a mature practice where the tasks and challenges will become second nature to you. It is understandable that you might be impatient, or that your confidence may be a little fragile.

Most counselling and psychotherapy training requires clinical practice or placement as part of the requirement for qualification, so you may already have some of the practical skills necessary to meet and work with clients. These skills were developed during your training, and will continue to develop throughout your practising life. Likewise, the skills of growing and running a successful practice will develop over time. However, the two sets of skills are very different. It will help you greatly in the future to understand that basic concept. This e-book does not primarily address the clinical practice skills although I do occasionally refer to more clinical issues.

For those of you who have had to find clients or placements for yourselves during the training process, you will have had a taster of the business side of the journey ahead of you. However, even if you already have some clients, I hope you will find some ideas here to help you. This book focuses in the main on practice development and management issues. It is about the business skills and knowledge you need to establish and run your practice.

The book should also be useful for therapists who are already in practice and are seeking ways to expand their practices, or develop their management skills.

It is often said about therapy that there is no destination, although it may seem that there is. Establishing yourself in this business is something you can start in a couple of days, and then spend the rest of your life at. It's a process. So relax and enjoy the journey.

As you start, if you have not already done so, spend a little time thinking about how you would like it to work out for you. What is your dream? Later in this book, we'll do an exercise to help you tease it out a little.

Therapy Work is Special

Working as a therapist is different from other occupations.

There are dilemmas and concerns peculiar to the work that are not relevant in other professions. Some therapists believe that these dilemmas restrict us when it comes to seeing a therapy practice as a business. In part 9 of this book I discuss some of these Dilemmas Peculiar to Therapy Practice, and the impact they may have on our ability to earn a living from the work.

The challenge for a therapist starting their own practice is to engage with the ways of the business world to the extent needed to create a financially viable practice. Sometimes, addressing the clinical issues can be elevated to a plane above the business ones. This book talks little of the clinical issues, but I am not dismissing or denying them.

That is not what this book is about.

As you read this book, be alert to where you might feel resistance arising for you. Be gentle with yourself. It's a process. Take the steps slowly. Introduce and integrate one piece before moving on to the next.

Preparing The Ground

As I said, the start-up phase of creating your practice will take at least two to three years. Why so long? It takes time for you to develop the sources of work, create processes that support you, and get used to the various day-to-day tasks that are an integral part of running your own business. It also takes some time to create and develop a momentum that will carry you on through the years ahead.

If things go according to plan, and your practice grows as you want it to, then you are likely to have more time to think about some of these issues *now* than later, when you have more clients. Also, once your practice is up and running, you will find it more difficult to change the way you operate. So, make the most of this opportunity while you can.

Use this time to create a vision of the sort of practice you'd like to have. Think about the sort of clients you'd like to attract, where you'd like to practice, and the sort of work that appeals to you. Imagine yourself five or ten years from now, and what you might like to have achieved by then. I will come back to this point later in this chapter.

Also, consider using this time to sort out some of the practical administrative and promotional issues. You could set up a bookkeeping system, a system for creating and retaining client notes, start a database of potential sources of income, and make contact with other professionals from whom you might hope to receive some work. We'll look at these issues again in detail later in the book: see Getting Started: Basic Housekeeping Tasks and Getting Started: Getting Those First Clients in Part 2.

Walking Two Roads: The Internal and the External Journeys

We walk two journeys in life, the internal journey and the

external one. On the external journey, we are concerned with what we do and how we do it. We turn ideas into action and thoughts into reality. We interact with our environment, and with other people. The internal journey is how we think about what we do or want to do, and how we feel about it. In life, we travel these two roads at the same time, a bit like being in both lanes of the dual carriageway at once!

In practising as a therapist or counsellor, it is the same. There are the practical things we do as a therapist and counsellor, the interventions we make with our clients, the everyday tasks of starting and finishing sessions, receiving money and writing up notes. And then there's the internal piece of how we feel and think about doing them.

Our training focuses in large measure on bringing us into our own internal journey, in preparation for inviting our future clients into theirs. We begin to understand how our experiences growing up and in early adulthood can have echoes in our present. We begin to see how our values and beliefs can both support and undermine our ability to meet the world. We sit with our clients and support them as they touch these aspects of themselves.

Many clients live their lives largely in the external journey, and therapy may be the only time in their week where they take time out to visit their thoughts and feelings. However, for many therapists themselves, in their work or their lives, the opposite applies. I come from a background in accountancy, a profession that is very much focused on action. My subsequent training as a therapist was a huge contrast to my previous occupation, as I learned to reflect at length on my feelings, my motives, and my underlying patterns and beliefs. This latter process is now so ingrained that there have been times when I can get stuck in my internal world and find it hard to take action.

At other times, the internal journey has also been an escape for me. Sometimes, it is easier to stay in the thoughts and feelings a situation has evoked than it is to take the appropriate action. I can manipulate how I look at and feel about the situation, and I can create a reason not to change it. I imagine that many of you may relate to this.

We always have choices about how we meet the experience of our lives. Some situations call for an internal response, some an external one, and sometimes we need both. While exploring how we feel may change our view or our relationship with our circumstances, at some stage in the process we also need to engage with life at a practical level. If we are hungry, we can reflect on our hunger, we can ask ourselves about its origins, we can explore how we feel about it, but these choices will not satisfy unless we also go to the fridge and eat something.

My emphasis in this book may go against some of the learning that helped you qualify as a therapist. The balance of emphasis here is towards strategy, planning and execution, and away from taking as much time as you need to get to know yourself better. I'm not saying that your internal process is not important, of course it is. But it is not the main focus of this book.

What Makes a Practice Successful?

What differentiates those who are still in practice years after they start from those who aren't? Many therapists who set out to run their own practice give up within the first three years. What makes the difference? Are those who fail less able at what they do? Are they less competent, skillful or caring therapists? NO!

What differentiates one group from the other is largely the ability to integrate the two perspectives we work from. Our feelings, mindset and attitude on the one hand, and our ability to take appropriate action on the other.

Those who succeed in developing and running a thriving therapy practice tend to be able to move between these two perspectives; standing back and reflecting when appropriate, and moving into action when action is needed and timely.

Where Do You Need To Go From Here?

My intention in this book is to provide guidance and support to you to create the practice and the income that you would like. Most therapists I speak to feel their work is rewarding. So do I. It is hugely satisfying to see a client recovering from an ordeal, making more of their life, healing an old trauma or developing more enjoyable relationships.

However, I hear from some colleagues their disappointment, and their resignation, that the cost of qualifying and practising is high, financially, emotionally and physically. Many struggle to maintain an income that supports them. Some have decided that that's just the way it is. Others have accepted that doing the work is what's important to them, and some feel that earning more would in some way compromise what they want to do.

My wish for you is that your experience of the business side of your practice will give you satisfaction too. To achieve this you will need to have some business and management skills. I'd like to help you with that. I'd like this book to help you to grow your practice into one that suits you, your values and your needs.

What Do You Want To Get From Your Practice?

The first step in starting a therapy or counselling practice is to ask yourself what you want your practice to be like. Since I've yet to meet someone who consciously sets out to fail, I am assuming that you want your practice to be a success. Later in this book, I'll introduce you to the Six Pillars that support a successful, thriving practice. Throughout this book, I'll give you some practical ideas to help you to move towards a more satisfying experience of the business of therapy. However, at this stage, I'd like you to think a bit more about what you want to get from your practice.

Sometimes, having qualified, people rush into practice as the next obvious step. However, it may not be the best choice for you. So an important question to ask yourself is, "What do I want to get from this?" as the answer will shape the type of practice you want to create. Some possible answers might be:

- Being employed, full or part time

- Supplementing other income

- Providing a social service

- Making a contribution

- Passing on a gift you received

- Keeping occupied and involved or having a hobby

Before committing yourself to something which you soon realise is not sustainable, it's really worthwhile to look at some of these questions in depth. Perhaps you are clear that you want to do this work and that you really want to help clients, but have never thought about the best way for you to go about that. If you have never been self-employed before, you might want to read Part 4: The First Pillar: Owning Your Practice, before going any further. Being self-employed is very different from being an employee, and before committing yourself further, you need to be very clear that that's what's right for you.

I'm assuming if you are continuing to read, that you are

satisfied that this is the right route for you. The next step then is to spend a little time exploring ...

What Would A Thriving Practice Look Like For You?

How would you know that your practice is successful?

- A client who turns their life around?

- Having lots of clients?

- Getting a good income from your work?

- An ability to identify what your client is struggling with and having some idea about   how to help them?

- A certificate from a college or university confirming your qualification?

- Receiving referrals through former or current clients?

- Other therapists asking for your advice and support?

- Never being the subject of a disciplinary or legal action?

- A deep feeling of satisfaction from your work?

- A sense of privilege that you have met another person at their most vulnerable?

Each of us will have a different idea of what success will look like. Maybe some or all, or maybe none of these things will ring true for you. Having an idea of what success means for you will help to shape your decisions and your actions. It will also help you to recognise it when you achieve it!

Focusing on these questions helps us to identify what is really important to us. This is not always an easy task. For example, when I ask myself which of the above criteria is most important for me, I find it differs according to my mood, or whether I have enough money to meet my bills. It may be influenced by something I heard or read recently or by someone I spoke to. But that's okay too. For now, a general idea of what we'd like to achieve will suffice to get us going.

Exercise: Imagine Your Future Practice

Imagine yourself in practice five years from now.

If you are just setting out on this journey, and your practice is still an idea rather than reality, ask yourself what you'd like to achieve in that period. How would you like your practice to look five years from now?

If you are already in practice, how will your practice be different five years from now?

- How many clients would you like to see each week or month?
- What issues would you like to be dealing with?
- Would you like to be working with long-term or short-term clients? Or a mixture?
- Will your clients be of a particular age or gender?
- What days or hours would you like to work?
- What income would you like to have?

- How will you see yourself as a therapist?

- Where will your practice be based? Will you work alone or with other therapists?

- Would you like to be working face to face, by phone or Internet?

- What additional training or experience would you like to have done?

These are just examples to help you create a picture of the future practice you'd like to have.

I'll explore some of these questions in more depth further on in this book, to help you get started on creating a vision of what's right for you. And your initial ideas will change and develop as you gain more confidence and experience. As you read, take some notes of ideas that resonate with you, and also those for which you have a strong negative response. Both give you good information, about your preferences, your set-points and your resistance.

Part 2:

Setting Up In Practice For The First Time

A Quick-Start Guide

If you don't have time to read the whole book now, this chapter will give you all the basics you need to get started straight away. It includes the basic housekeeping tasks you need to perform, the things you need to think about in finding somewhere to work, thoughts about finding those first few clients, important steps in looking after yourself, and, if you get stuck, some ideas about getting past the roadblocks.

Getting Started: Basic Housekeeping Tasks

When setting up a self-employed practice, there are some practical "housekeeping" things you need to do. Here's a checklist to get you started.

1. **Register the name of your practice with the Companies Registration Office** if your practice name is anything other than your "true" name. (Read more about naming and registering your practice in Part 5: What's In a Name?)

2. **Open a dedicated bank account for your practice.** Lodge all receipts, and pay all practice expenses out of this account. This makes preparing your accounts at year end so much simpler.

3. **Inform your Tax Office**: It is your responsibility to inform the Revenue Commissioners that you have commenced to practice, even if you don't initially expect to have a tax liability. The onus is on you to ensure that returns are

submitted and any tax paid; it is not up to the Revenue to find and assess you. In Ireland, Income Tax returns are due and income tax payable on 31st October each year. (Read more about this subject in Part 7:Tax Returns.)

4. **Put your insurance in place**: You will need to have both Professional Indemnity Insurance and Public Liability Insurance. Your home insurance may need to be amended if you are going to practise from your home. Consider also whether you need income protection insurance (covering you for extended illness) and a pension.

5. **Check for any requirements of your professional body**: Advise your professional body that you've started to practise and provide any additional information they require. If your professional body publishes an online directory of practising members for the public, make sure your profile is updated.

6. **Find somewhere to work.** Issues to consider include:

   - The suitability (Is it quiet, private, comfortable?)

   - The cost (Rental on an hourly basis will cost a little more than renting for a block of hours)

   - Safety (Is the premises or the car park secure, especially at night?)

   - Location (Is it convenient for you and your

clients?)

- Privacy (Is it suitably discreet?).

In the short term, you may decide to accept a less than perfect solution to carry you until you become established. (Read more below and in Part 5: Home or Away: Where to Set Up Your Practice.)

7. **Decide on a fee level:** What you charge and how you charge it will be influenced by how much income you need, how many hours you have to give, and how much you expect to pay in expenses. (Read more at Part 9: Setting a Fee Level.)

8. **Create a Budget:** Estimate your income and expenses for the first year to give you a rough idea of whether you need additional capital by way of a loan or savings. (Read more at Part 9: Budgeting And Cash Flow.)

9. **Start your bookkeeping:** At a minimum, record details of your income and your expenditure, and keep the relevant receipts and invoices. Learn what expenses you will be allowed to deduct from income for tax purposes, see Revenue.ie for details or ask a financial advisor. Typically, expenses incurred *wholly, exclusively and necessarily* for the purposes of your practice will be allowed. (Read more in Part 7: Practice Books And Records.)

10. **Arrange your supervision:** Check any requirements of

your professional body such as hours and accreditation. (Read more in Part 8: Supervision.)

11. **Hire any professional advisors:** For example, you may decide you need an accountant to complete and submit your accounts and tax returns to the Revenue Commissioners, or a solicitor to advise on legal aspects.

Getting Started: Finding Somewhere To Practise From

One of the first decisions when starting a practice is where to locate yourself. There are many choices available, although it may not seem like that. Here are some ideas to think about, and to help you choose:

- **Home or Away:** If you have space and your family circumstances allow for it, working from home can be a good, low-cost option. You will save on travel time, have more flexibility about appointment times, and you will have no rent to pay. There are also some downsides. These include having to keep the space clean and orderly and relatively well maintained. There may be some impact on your privacy. Working from home may also affect the tax status of your home. (Read more at Part 5: Home or Away: Where to Set Up Your Practice.)

- **Alone or with Others:** Having a space that you don't share with other people means you can have it the way you want it, and you have total flexibility about the times you choose to work. However, unless you are seeing a large number of clients, it's probably an expensive option. When others share your space, the room may be rearranged by them or you may have delays in crossover times. If you only want to work a small number of hours, it's more cost effective to share. You have the added bonus of meeting other practitioners, even briefly, between sessions. (Read more at Part 5: Working By Yourself Or With Others?)

- **Cost Structure:** Different arrangements apply in different locations. Some rooms are rented out by the hour, for some you have to buy a block of time. Buying by the hour, where you pay only for the hours booked and used, will probably work out cheaper, even though the per-hour rate may be higher than you would pay for a block. However, renting a block of time, where you pay for the time whether you use it or not, gives more flexibility and security, as you can add clients without having to check availability.

- **Convenience vs. Population:** It may be conveniently located for you, but what about your potential clients? Is it located near a centre of population, where clients may be found? Is it easy to find? Is there room for people to park easily?

- **Ambience / Atmosphere:** Does the energy in the room suit you and the way you work? Do you feel comfortable there? What do you like, friendly and relaxed, or calm and professional? Do you like to talk with your colleagues, or do you prefer a strictly enforced quiet rule? Do you like to hear music playing or the sound of a water feature? How about outside noises?

- **Is There a Genuine Gap in the Market or Just No Market?** Are other therapy or counselling practices located in an area that you're considering? Perhaps there is a gap in the market, and this may be an opportunity for you. Or it may indicate that there is no interest in the area for the type of work you're doing. Existing practices may indicate some level of familiarity and acceptance locally about the service you are providing. If there are no practices, you may have to convince potential referrers and clients of the value of what you are offering.

- **Privacy:** Is the location discreet? Privacy is a big issue for some clients. Others will be comfortable with being seen entering a counselling or therapy practice. Clients differ.

- **Potential for Growth:** When you're first establishing yourself, getting clients is a priority. Does the location you're considering have potential as a client source? Working as part of a centre with other therapists or healing professionals may have the advantage of situations in which colleagues can pass potential clients to you.

- **Other Bonuses:** Some centres will provide peer or other supervision, training, or emergency cover as part of the contract.

Where Do You Find A Room? Think Creatively

1. Your local **church, community centre or library** may have rooms available either free or to rent.

2. **Doctors, other therapists or alternative health providers** may be willing to rent you space. They may also be willing to send you referrals.

3. **Serviced offices** can be rented on a daily or hourly basis. Individual office units within a block may be available. Check with local estate agents.

4. **Related small retail businesses** such as **health food shops, holistic or yoga centres** may have free space at the back or above the shop that they may be willing to rent.

5. Use a room in your own or someone else's home. **Someone who lives alone and has a free room may be willing to rent** to you. Check the advertisements in local magazines and papers.

6. Check the notice boards in **supermarkets, shopping centres, credit unions,** etc. They often carry advertisements for locally available rooms to rent. You could also consider placing an advertisement there yourself looking for a room.

7. Check with your **professional body**. Their journal or

website may carry classified ads offering rooms to rent. Again, you could place an ad here yourself.

8. Take an ad on **Facebook** or Google. A small investment may be effective with an ad targeted towards those most likely to be able to help.

9. **Pick up the phone and ring therapists you know**, ask if they have a room they'd be willing to rent to you. If they don't, ask do they know of one to rent. Ask friends and family even if they aren't therapists. This is how I found the first place I practised from.

10. Be open to **creative ideas.** Maybe you could convert a shed or a caravan. If someone can live in a metal shipping container, perhaps you could use one as a therapy room!

11. **Go virtual**, and practise over the phone or on Skype/FaceTime. Make your practice mobile, and visit clients in their own homes. Or make an outside space your therapy room, and walk and talk.

Don't get stuck on the idea that this has to be a decision that works for the rest of your practising career. Focus on finding a solution in the short term. This gives you time to reflect on what you want long term. Your needs now will change as your practice develops, and what works when you're starting out may not fit in five, ten or twenty years' time.

Happy hunting!

Getting Started: Getting Those First Clients

So now that you have somewhere to practice and have started to put the building blocks in place, you need some clients to work with, some people who are in need of your help.

It helps if you know what sort of practice you'd like to have. Who are your clients going to be, and what services are you going to offer them? If these questions are difficult for you, or no ideas come to mind, you can read more about these issues in Part 5: The Second Pillar: Knowing Your Practice.

Marketing Yourself And Your Services

Finding clients means you have to promote yourself and your services to people who themselves need those services, or who come into contact with people who need those services. Having an idea of who your clients are likely to be will help to narrow the field for you. There's a saying that "if you're marketing to everyone, you're marketing to no-one." You can waste your time, your energy and your money promoting your services to people who don't need them, or who can't afford them.

Some therapists are hesitant to get too specific about the types of issues and clients they want to work with. They think that this will mean they are restricted to doing only that work. This is not what I am proposing. I am suggesting that you narrow your idea of a client to focus your marketing. You can choose to work with anyone you like.

Marketing your services where they are likely to be needed is simply adopting a more focused approach. For example, if working with children appeals to you, you can use that intention to shape how and where you market your services. You might focus your efforts towards parents, guardians, or teachers of children in difficulty and look for places you might find them such as schools or support groups. You can apply the same idea for any other work.

Conversely, when it comes to thinking about referrals, you should initially try to think as broadly as possible about who might be able to help you to get clients. GPs and other health professionals can certainly be a good source of work; however, don't confine your thoughts there, as many potential clients will not think of their doctor when facing a problem.

Your friends, family, or past and present work colleagues, other counsellors and anybody who works in a caring or helping role may be potential sources of referral for you. If you'd like to read more about this issue, visit my website http://www.thisbusinessoftherapy.com or http://tinyurl.com/h3xv49r to get your free copy of my report "Five Ways to Boost Your Therapy Practice."

So how do you let the right people know that you are ready to receive their business? There are many routes to getting your name out there where a client might find you:

- Business cards
- Advertisements in newspapers, magazines, or online

- Brochures and flyers

- Entries in professional and local directories, print and online

- Sponsorship of local events

- Articles in local newspapers or magazines

- Workshops, courses and presentations

- Your own website, and

- Social media

These are all ways in which practices can highlight their services. Have a look at what other counsellors, therapists and similar professions are doing. See what appeals to you, and what's not for you.

Differentiating Yourself

What should you say about yourself? It's useful to identify something that differentiates you from other practices providing similar services. This may be a particular qualification or skill you possess that perhaps others don't have. It might be your own personal story to which others may relate (for example, that you work with families who have lost someone to suicide, because of your own experience in this area). Perhaps your beliefs or values bring a particular flavour to your work, such as helping women who have experienced abortion. Find something about you that is different, and then you can use it directly or indirectly in marketing your practice. A relationship with clients starts from the first time they see your photo or hear your name. This may be long before they call you to make an appointment. What would you like them to know?

If putting yourself out there in this way is new to you, you may feel acutely uncomfortable as you start, and fear that everyone will be as focused on the detail of what you say or do as you are. Generally, the opposite is true. We live in an age where people are overwhelmed with information, and there are so many choices out there for those seeking help that you may have to become quite vocal to be heard. It may take some hustling to get those first few clients until you have established a reputation for yourself. So, if your first efforts to promote your services don't give you the return you expected, don't get too despondent! It will take time.

Getting Started: Looking After Yourself In The Work

Although not strictly a business issue, one of the most basic and fundamental things you need to remember when setting up in practice is the importance of self-care. In therapy practice, even at the best of times, there is a danger that the therapist's needs get pushed aside by the needs of her clients. The danger is especially acute starting up your own practice when you have worked as an employee previously. Not only is everything new and strange, but until a constant stream of work is established, every client hour may be vital to your financial situation. So you need to be vigilant, and to put in place some safeguards to look after yourself.

Luckily, there are some straightforward ways to look after yourself so that you are fully able to provide what your clients need:

1. Be aware of your own needs, physical, emotional, psychological and financial. Provide a good service to your clients, but balance their needs against your own. You cannot give to your clients when you have no resources yourself. You also can't help everyone who needs help, nor should you. Remember, and encourage your clients to remember, that they have other supports in their life apart from you.

2. Notice the impact your clients have on you, and if it becomes overwhelming, take steps to address it. For example, you may wish to spend some time arranging the chairs in the room at a distance that suits you, or find a way to break the tension, by reaching for a glass of water or briefly leaving the room. If you find yourself left with feelings after a session, you might want to take longer breaks between clients to give yourself time to recover.

3. Appreciate what you provide for your client. If you find it hard to charge a fair value for your work you may want to reflect on that with your supervisor or therapist. It took time, energy and money to acquire your qualification, and you shouldn't work for nothing

just because a client has financial difficulties. Valuing yourself and your work is not only self-care but also makes an important statement about your willingness to be appreciated, in which you model something that will benefit your clients.

4. Listen to your own needs and desires. One of the big benefits of being self-employed is that you can decide what works best for you. Stand up for what's important to you, whether it's taking holidays, working particular hours or with particular issues, or being clear about saying "No."

5. Establish firm boundaries, including your preferences for fees, cancellations and no-shows. You make the rules that are right for you. Honour your own choices, and don't cave in just because it doesn't suit a client. If these issues are hard for you, a written contract may help. You'll find an example at Appendix 2.

6. Pay attention to your physical needs such as exercising, taking appropriate breaks and rests, and eating well. Engage in practices that help you to manage the stress and impact of the work, such as yoga, meditation or mindfulness. (One of my favourites is EFT.) Even doing some deep breathing for a few minutes can feel like a mini break. These are basics, but often forgotten!

7. Allow yourself to decide whether you really want to

work with a client or not, and support yourself in that choice. It's okay to say "No." A "Yes" has little meaning if you can't say "No." In the long term, you'll feel angry and resentful. Get to know what suits and doesn't suit you in the work. As you gradually give more space to your preferences, the work will be less stressful.

8. Allow others to support you. Stay in touch with colleagues and friends. Reach out to people who can understand what you do, and how it affects you. Spend your free time with people who are easy and undemanding to be around, and who don't need you to take care of them.

Your investment in self-care will pay off. You'll reduce the likelihood of stress-related illness, compassion fatigue or burnout. Don't forget that you are the most valuable asset in your practice, so treat yourself accordingly!

Getting Started: Resistance, Procrastination And Excuses

Starting any small business is a daunting prospect, and starting a therapy practice is no exception. If you have never worked for yourself before, it can be a particularly steep learning curve. And so, if you find yourself backtracking and coming up with all sorts of reasons why this is not a good time to do this, be gentle with yourself. It is natural to feel like that, and anyone who has gone before you will understand it.

What we resist persists. And that is as true of our procrastination as it is of anything else. Trying to force yourself past your resistance will probably just create more resistance down the road. Maybe your hesitation is trying to tell you something. Maybe this is the wrong time, maybe you're not ready to take this step. Perhaps you need more supports in place (either practical or emotional) before moving forward. Ask yourself, "What would help me to take the next step?"

Go gently with yourself, we need to respect our own resistance to change. Accept that's where you're at and that it will change in time. This one step alone is often enough to open space for something to change. If the resistance persists, you may need to get some support from outside. I offer a free 20-minute consultation to anyone with a question, query or problem. You can email me here: jude.fay@thisbusinessoftherapy.com Perhaps talking about it may help?

One or more of the following ideas might also help:

Start with an objective. What is your goal for your practice? Try getting specific about some of the details, such as when would you like to be up and running, and how would you like it to look? For example, when my friend and colleague Jennifer and I were setting up, we spent quite a bit of time mulling over the various options that were open to us. I wanted us to have a front door of our own, the atmosphere to be warm and friendly, somewhere there would be contact with other therapists or like-minded professionals. Thinking about it in advance really paid off, because when opportunities arose, we were both really clear about whether they were right for us, or were a step to where we wanted to be. To help with this step, re-read Preparing The Ground in Part 1 of this book. Notice what draws you or where you get stuck!

Start Early and Plan Ahead: The law of the harvest says it takes time for things to grow. A seed put in the ground today won't become a tree overnight. Most people can't decide to establish themselves in practice today and open up tomorrow. It could be as long as six months before all the pieces are in place. (See Getting Started: Basic Housekeeping Tasks earlier in this chapter.) It takes time to put promotional materials together, and it takes time for your marketing efforts to translate into paying clients. It takes time to make contact with and arrange to meet doctors or other sources of referral. Make it easy for yourself by starting to think about these things long before you need to put them into practice. Recognise that it will take time, and don't put yourself under unnecessary pressure. Ensure you have some supports (emotional and financial) in place while you undergo the early stages.

Have an Accountability Buddy: I can't emphasise enough how much easier it is when you go through this process with someone else. If you know someone else who is setting up, or has recently set up, make contact and ask whether they'd be open to you being a support/accountability buddy for each other. You don't need any connection other than the common ground of setting up or developing your practice.

You'll find it helps to have someone you can voice your commitments to, make deadlines for tasks, share information, and support you when you get wobbly (and if you're like me, boy, will you get wobbly!!) Pick someone who will hip-check you if you don't deliver. If the procrastination gets out of hand, try having a penalty and reward system for yourself. For example, "I'll do this task now, and then I'll have a break to read my book." Or, "If I don't do it today, I'll give you €20."

My current accountability buddy is a health and wellness coach who lives in Australia. We met through an online workshop, and although we have never met in person, we have kept in regular contact. We encourage and support each other to move towards our goals.

Persistence: Napoleon Hill wrote in his classic book *Think and Grow Rich*[1] that lack of persistence is one of the major causes of failure. In his view, most failures (in any area of life) occur not because people are unable to get what they want, but because they give up too soon. Maybe they want it all to go without any challenges and then see any setbacks as evidence that they shouldn't be trying to do it at all. So take heart, and be patient and persistent. It might not happen the way you expect it to, or at the time you'd like it to, but this does not mean it's not going to happen at all.

When I first took on clients in training, two of the first three clients did not come for more than one session, and the third came only for two sessions. None of them told me they were not continuing. I could have given up at that stage because the negative critic in my head was telling me I was completely unsuited to this line of work. I might well have given up were it not for the structure and support of the training course around me. Since then there have been many, many occasions when I have felt like quitting, because of things that have gone wrong. Knowing that I had another person alongside me in the process helped me to keep going when the going got tough.

Remember, procrastination, resistance and excuses are all fear based. You can spend forever exploring and getting to the root of them. You can analyse them, justify them, and explain them, but they will never bring a paying client to your door. You can't learn to swim by reading a book sitting beside the swimming pool. Eventually, you're going to have to get wet. Do yourself a favour, DO IT NOW!

Exercise: Do It Now!

It's very tempting just to keep reading; I know, I've been there. However, it's important to move into action too. So ... Start your commitment to yourself and your practice right now.

Re-read this chapter and choose five small tasks you can do without any further background or information. Get a piece of paper and write the numbers 1 to 5 down the left-hand side. Beside the number 1, write today's date and one of the small tasks. Beside number 2, write tomorrow's date and another small task, and so on until you have dates for the next five days, with a task next to each. It might look like this:

1. (Today) List possible sources of work.

2. (Tomorrow) Ring one person I know and tell them what I'm doing.

3. (Next day) Look on the Internet for local rooms to rent.

4. (Next day) Get Professional Indemnity and Personal Liability Insurance.

5. (Next day) Draft a letter to local GPs announcing my service.

Try and have a mix of tasks, involving housekeeping items and promotional items. Each day, you have two tasks to do: the task for that day on the list you've created, PLUS adding one more task to the end of the list.

By having a rolling list of tasks, you get into the habit of working ON your business each day. If you can't do the next task on the list, or you feel a huge push back against it, pass over that one for now, and move to the next one.

SIX PILLARS OF A
SUCCESSFUL THERAPY PRACTICE

OWNING YOUR PRACTICE	GOALS	KEY TASKS	KEY MINDSET
	Ownership, Commitment, Responsibly, Authority, Purpose,	Putting the basic building blocks in place	Willingness to take action, Willingness to Take risks

KNOWING YOUR PRACTICE	GOALS	KEY TASKS	KEY MINDSET
	Identity, Vision	Creating a business plan	Willingness to make choices and decisions

GROWING YOUR PRACTICE	GOALS	KEY TASKS	KEY MINDSET
	Survival, Longevity and Prosperity	Getting out there	Willingness to be seen

MANAGING YOUR PRACTICE	GOALS	KEY TASKS	KEY MINDSET
	Order and Harmony, Smooth Running	Create processes and structure	Discipline

MINDING YOUR PRACTICE	GOALS	KEY TASKS	KEY MINDSET
	Safeguarding, Security, Support	Identify and manage risks	Willingness to create and hold boundries

VALUING YOUR PRACTICE	GOALS	KEY TASKS	KEY MINDSET
	Flourishing, Reward, Satisfaction	Financial management and planning	Self-worth, willingness to receive

Part 3:

Six Pillars Of A Successful Therapy Practice

However you'd like your future counselling or therapy practice to be, there are six essential pillars that you need to consider. These are:

- Owning Your Practice

- Knowing Your Practice

- Growing Your Practice

- Managing Your Practice

- Minding Your Practice

- Valuing Your Practice

Each of these pillars supports your practice. Each has a different goal and different tasks that need to be done to ensure your practice is standing on a secure foundation. If one is a bit wobbly, well, it would be like a table with a wobbly leg! Each one also needs a certain mindset or attitude to help carry it through.

I will introduce each of the pillars here, and will continue to refer to them throughout the book.

The First Pillar – Owning Your Practice

Goals: Ownership, commitment, responsibility, authority, purpose

Key tasks: Putting the basic building blocks in place

Key mindset: Willingness to take action, willingness to take risks

The goal of the first pillar is to take ownership of your practice. Ownership is mindset supported by action. We demonstrate our ownership by taking the actions that need to be taken, knowing that the actions will take us closer to the goals we have set. We take responsibility for our practice and for ourselves. We commit to being in practice, not just in the service of our clients, but in the service of ourselves too.

There are things that must be done in the service of the work and in the interest of the client, even if we don't like doing them. I don't think I've ever met or spoken to a therapist who is not fully committed to their clients. But it is much harder to make choices that serve ourselves and our own needs, particularly if those needs impact on the needs of others. (And I'll let you in on a secret, I find it just as hard as you do!)

Everyone will find some aspects of starting up and running a practice particularly difficult. Common ones include promoting our work, asking for a fair fee or making tough decisions. These challenges and the fears that they evoke can keep us stuck in a place of not committing fully or taking ownership of our practices. I suspect you can relate to this dynamic where there are competing objectives at play, the objective to move forward and grow, and the objective to stay safe. And both are important.

The first pillar of a successful therapy practice, Owning Your Practice, embraces both of these objectives. It is not really a pillar in the sense that it actually supports the other pillars; it is very much about mindset, about choosing to embody and act from our adult rather than our child selves. Just as piloting a boat takes a different skill set from driving a car, owning your own practice, whatever its size, takes a very different mindset from being employed by someone else. In Part 4: The First Pillar: Owning Your Practice we'll look at some of the skills and habits that we need to have, and how they differ from those needed to be an employee or work within an organisation.

The Second Pillar – Knowing Your Practice

Goals: Identity, vision

Key tasks: Creating a business plan

Key mindset: Willingness to make choices and decisions

The second pillar is concerned with identity. Therapists are familiar with the search for and importance of identity, either in their own lives, or their clients' lives. When it comes to having your own therapy practice, being clear about who you are is equally important whether you are meeting with your clients, or developing and managing your practice. This involves decisions and choices about who you are as a practitioner and also who you are not. It involves decisions about what you stand for, and what is important to you.

How much do you really know the *business* of being a therapist? When you hear the word *business* in the context of being a therapist and starting a practice, how do you relate to it? What is evoked in you? I'm sure you could tell me all about your clients, about their problems, their relationships, their attitudes and their temperaments. Equally, I have no doubt that even as you begin your professional career, your ability to work with those clients is strong. But do you know as much about the *business* of starting and running a professional practice?

Of course it is important that you know your clients and how to be and to work with them. However, knowing your practice involves more than that. It also involves knowledge and understanding of the profession, the market and the area in which your practice will operate. It involves knowing what changes may affect your practice and the laws and regulations that govern you. It means knowing what makes a client choose you and your service rather than going for Reiki or anti-depressants. Knowing more about these issues will better equip you to make choices that will work for you.

A business plan is the medium through which you begin to bring your ideas into reality, and to put flesh on the bones of your vision. By starting to identify the specifics of what you're trying to achieve in your practice, you start to turn your thoughts into things. This means making choices and decisions about how you are going to proceed.

The Third Pillar – Growing Your Practice

Goals: Survival, longevity and prosperity

Key tasks: Getting out there

Key mindset: Willingness to be seen

To share your skills and presence with others, to do what you have trained long and hard to do, you need to have clients; ideally, enough clients to create a robust and viable practice which can withstand the ups and downs that inevitably come along. This means being willing to let others see you, and willing to be proud of what you have to offer. It's a myth that being good at what you do is enough. If you have another income and years of patience, you can wait for clients to come to you organically, but it will be very slow.

If a business is not growing, it's stagnating or declining. Like everything else on this planet, it is in a constant cycle of change. If you don't weed your garden and cut the grass, nature will soon take its toll. Without some attention, leaves will fall and the wasps will eat your fruit, so it doesn't stay the same for long. Likewise, you can't create a practice and then leave it to its own devices. You need to put some time and energy into it, especially in the early days.

Clients come and go, so it is a constant cycle of death and re-birth. That means your practice will really benefit from regular encouragement to grow. When you are more established some work will come in of its own accord, but to ensure that you don't have to endure long periods of lower income with the feelings of uncertainty and insecurity that may arise, you need to have a plan to attract the work you need.

Any promotion is better than none, but infrequently making a huge sprint is usually less effective than little and often. A frequent reminder places your name up front in people's minds so that when they have a client to refer or they are looking for a therapist or counsellor, it's you they turn to.

You don't need to be "pushy" or "salesy" to promote your services. There are lots of ways to promote your practice. What works will be different for each of us. There's no right way to do it. Find something that works for you and keep doing it.

If promoting your work and your practice is something that's new for you, it might be best to keep it simple. Choose one activity from those set out in Part 6: The Third Pillar: Growing Your Practice and commit to it for at least three months, devoting a manageable amount of time to it on a regular basis. One action taken consistently is better than a dozen actions that are taken randomly and sporadically. There are lots of ideas about how to market your practice in this book, and if you'd like more, check out some of the articles on my website thisbusinessoftherapy.com, for example, "Five Ways To Make Your Marketing More Effective" at http://tinyurl.com/jmmvskd

The Fourth Pillar – Managing Your Practice

Goals: Order and harmony, smooth running

Key tasks: Create processes and structure

Key mindset: Discipline

The fourth pillar is where the housekeeping gets done, the books get written up, the toilets get cleaned, and the cat gets fed. You don't have to bury yourself in rigidity, but some structure and order is essential. This takes discipline.

Managing any business is very much a mindset thing. It's not just a question of knowing what to do, and when it should be done, you also need to decide what to do, and then either do it or ensure that it gets done.

Starting and running a business involves action. Your practice will require attention, thinking about and maintenance. At all times, there will be little chores to be done such as bills to be paid, insurance to be put in place, rooms to be cleaned, supplies to be bought for the bathroom and the kitchen, diary or bookings to be managed, the books to be written up and tax returns prepared. And that dripping tap needs to be fixed. None of these tasks are overwhelming, but they don't go away because we don't want to engage with them. It helps if you can be organised about it!

The Fifth Pillar – Minding Your Practice

Goals: Safeguarding, security, support

Key tasks: Identify and manage risks

Key mindset: Willingness to create and set boundaries

The fifth pillar of a successful practice brings a delicate sense of balance to the six-pillar structure. Where the first pillar was concerned with a willingness to take risks, the fifth pillar is concerned with managing risks through creating appropriate boundaries. The goal of this pillar is to safeguard the practice and its most valuable asset – you.

I'm sure you wouldn't leave your front door unlocked at night, or your wallet or handbag lying in the road, would you? There are several aspects to minding your practice. The most obvious one is making sure that the appropriate insurance is in place to safeguard you and your clients, i.e. public liability and professional indemnity. However, have you thought about insurance to protect your income in case you can't work? Do you have arrangements in place to let your clients know if something happens to you? Have you made a will or provided for your retirement?

Minding your business also includes making sure that you are complying with the appropriate laws, rules and regulations. These include the regulations of your professional body, and health and safety requirements.

An area where some practitioners fall down is self-care. There is a danger of putting clients' needs before the therapist's own. This can result in no longer being able to work, because they're sick, exhausted, burnt out or suffering from compassion fatigue. Minding your practice means looking after yourself before attending to the needs of your clients.

The Sixth Pillar – Valuing Your Practice

Goals: Flourishing, reward, satisfaction

Key tasks: Financial management and planning

Key mindset: Self-worth, willingness to receive

The sixth pillar is one that is difficult for many therapists. The difficulty lies in objectively seeing our value, not just in what we have to offer others, but also in our intrinsic value as human beings. It raises the spectre of placing a monetary value on our services, and since we are so closely identified with the service we provide, by extension, the notion that we are putting a monetary value on ourselves. This is tricky.

Training in counselling and psychotherapy is expensive. It costs money, time, and can be emotionally challenging. Also, you have lived your life and learned from your experiences. You have a lot to offer your clients. Can you own that?

Even with a qualification and accreditation it can be hard to own our value. Valuing your practice asks of you that you respect what you have to offer, and reflect a fair value on that through your fee. It means seeing your own needs and desires as important. It means having respect for your own values and boundaries, for example, about fees, cancellations and no-shows. Valuing yourself also means seeing your mistakes as part of the process and being kind and compassionate to yourself.

Going Forward

This chapter has been a brief introduction to the six pillars of a successful therapy practice. I hope it will help you to think more specifically about your therapy or counselling practice as a business. As we go through this book, I'll be referring to each pillar in more depth.

If you're already in practice, in respect of each of the areas we've considered, how well do you think your practice is doing? Which areas are you an ace at? And in which do you think you could usefully stretch and grow? Do you spend more time reflecting on and examining your thoughts and feelings, or do you rush into action without due consideration?

Exercise: Strengths And Growing Edges

Have a look at the "Therapy Practice Business Assessment" which you'll find on my website at http://tinyurl.com/zdfull5 to see which area you most need to focus on.

Part 4:

The First Pillar: Owning Your Practice

OWNING

"Ownership: 'A commitment of the head, heart, and hands to fix the problem and never again affix the blame." [2]

Goals: Ownership, commitment, responsibility, authority, purpose

Key tasks: Putting the basic building blocks in place

Key mindset: Willingness to take action, willingness to take risks

Not all those who train in this work go on to set up in practice. Still fewer practise on a full-time or exclusive basis (i.e., they have no other source of income.) In an IACP survey of members[3] in 2013, just 29% of those surveyed worked full time as a therapist, and 44% had another source of income. Of those surveyed, 45% responded that the "recession / personal finance or getting clients" was their greatest challenge.

What separates those who succeed in growing a viable practice from those who don't?

You might be surprised to learn that it's probably not their skill or ability as a therapist, but their business mindset. For some, the notion of a business mindset conjures up images of the "bad guys" of the business world who will go to any lengths to make money. You don't need to be like that to run a private practice, but you do need to have at least some element of business perspective.

Author Michael Gerber, in his series of E-Myth[4] books, speaks of the *entrepreneur mindset*, and highlights the distinction that he draws between those who are successful in business and those who aren't.

The E-Myth he refers to in the title of his books is the entrepreneur myth that anyone who sets up in business is an entrepreneur. He then goes on to disprove this myth. Everyone, he says, who is in business spends time working IN the business. In the case of therapists, we all spend our time working with clients. However, *that* time is not spent attending to the needs of the practice, or of the therapist. And therein lies the difference that Gerber says distinguishes those who succeed in business from those that don't.

So, to follow his way of thinking, those who succeed in growing a thriving private practice spend time working ON and thinking ABOUT the business, i.e. attending to the needs of the therapy practice, and of the therapist. It's a fine distinction but one which is very important.

Below, I set out some of the characteristics that successful practitioners display. I find it curious that most therapists demonstrate these traits on a daily basis in their client work, but many find it hard to apply them to the business sides of their practice. (And by the way, this is not a phenomenon exclusive to therapists, Michael Gerber was writing about businesses generally.) You don't need to be a whiz at applying all of these attributes to your practice on day one, but an openness to growing into them will help you to create the mindset that is needed if your practice is going to survive in the short term, and to flourish in the longer term.

As you read the paragraphs below, try to keep an open mind.

Each of these attributes has both their positive and negative sides, so it's not a question of right and wrong, or judging yourself for not being able. Just note which words resonate with you, and which jar. These reactions may tell you where you need to explore how you feel about being a business owner.

Attributes Of Business Ownership

- Ability to see the practice as a business

- Willingness to promote yourself and your practice

- Ability to manage workflow (to adapt to ebbs and flows in work volumes)

- Ability to maintain an appropriate balance between client expectations/needs, your needs and the needs of the practice

- Willingness and ability to create reasonable profit and cash flow

- Ability to manage priorities

- Ability to manage relationships in the interests of all – with clients and others

- Ability and willingness to say "No" and hold appropriate boundaries

- Ability to see the bigger picture

- Willingness to be patient and compassionate towards

yourself when things inevitably don't go to plan

- Ability to know when you're out of your depth

- Willingness to ask for help

Commitment: I see commitment as intention supported by action. No one else is going to make developing and running your practice a priority in their life, no one is going to do it for you. So it's a question of seeing yourself in the driving seat. This may mean learning and practising the skills and mindset of *running a business*. I'm not saying you have to value earning money above the work you do with clients, of course not; I'm talking about creating a balance.

Being committed to your practice is not only about identifying and working with your client's therapeutic needs, but also being committed to seeing and working with your own needs and the needs of your practice, such as earning a living, minding yourself, and doing the administrative chores that come with any business. Many practitioners are generous when it comes to the time they spend working with clients (IN their practice) but find it harder to commit their efforts ON their practice (e.g., bringing in new work).

Planning: There's a saying that if you don't care where you go, any road will do. Planning is the bridge between creating an intention and taking action. One of the characteristics that mark out those who survive in practice is their willingness to create and implement a plan. A broad business plan (even if it's informal) setting out the purpose, vision and strategy for the practice will support you in making decisions, focusing your efforts, and knowing when remedial action is needed.

Apathy and fatalism can creep in when things don't go the way you'd like. There can be a temptation to blame external circumstances (e.g., the financial climate) for your disappointment. A clear idea of financial targets (ideally formalised in writing) is more likely to yield the results you want because it will prompt you to take action, and gives direction to your choices.

Persistence: Imagine a toddler learning to walk. They fall down loads of times until they get the hang of it. If, as a small child, you had fallen down and then given up saying, "I can't do that," or "I tried it and it didn't work," you'd still be crawling! Learning to walk involves first connecting with the desire to do it, building the muscles, finding the balance and practicing it until it works. Remember how long it took to train as a therapist? Well, you need to think about the development and management of your practice in the same way.

Learning the skills of running a small business is a process of education, coupled with trial and error. In my experience, particularly in the area of practice promotion, some therapists are reluctant to persist with a strategy beyond their first attempt. I don't know the reason for this (and no doubt we could analyse it endlessly), but it is not a trait that will serve you. If you want to develop a practice that is financially viable, you will need to become comfortable with the idea that it will require your ongoing attention and input.

Willingness to Go Beyond What's Familiar: When you were training to be a therapist you had to unlearn some old habits and learn some new ones. You might have found it hard, for example, not to jump in immediately with a solution to your client's problem, or to be a bit more assertive in challenging some aspect of the client's behaviour that wasn't serving them. Well, just as you were willing to stretch outside what was then familiar for you to do your training, you will need to do the same for the development and management of your practice. The skills you learnt as a therapist probably now come naturally to you, but they may be the opposite of what is needed to be successfully self-employed. Does this mean you have to be a different therapist? Not at all. You need to be flexible, to be able to move within your range, judge what is a priority at the time, and make a decision.

A good example is about being paid for your work. Say a potential client is struggling financially and so are you. It is your instinct to look after your client's needs. Your choices include changing the frequency of your sessions, working with them at a lower rate that may not be economical for you or referring them to a low-cost service. There's no right answer.

Which leads me to the next skill:

Decision Making: Starting and running your own business calls for a lot of decision making, and some of those decisions may be really big ones. You may have to consider leaving your day job, and while for some that might seem a very attractive prospect, few realise the sense of security and belonging that comes from being part of an organisation. You may have to make decisions that will have financial implications, like committing to a lease, or a contract to hire a room. You will have to decide what sort of room you want, and where you want that room to be. You will have to decide what services you are going to provide and what clients you'd like to work with. There will be decisions about how to market yourself and your practice, decisions about a name, a logo, and the colour of stationery. Each of these will raise issues with you and may challenge you in ways you do not expect.

Typically, when working for someone else, there will be limits to the decisions you have to make, and if you feel out of your depth, you can always ask a colleague, a manager or employer for help. While you can ask for the opinions and support of others in some of these decisions about setting up in practice, ultimately, you're the one who gets to decide. Depending on how you see risk that could feel like freedom, or could be seriously scary.

One way to help yourself with this is to get used to making small decisions where it doesn't matter. Choose a different way home, or a different type of coffee. Rearrange your sitting room (you can always change it back.) Listen to a different radio station or watch an unfamiliar TV show. Notice what comes up for you as you do this. Do you worry about making the wrong decision? Or perhaps what others might think? Do you find yourself endlessly weighing up the options, or moving quickly to avoid the discomfort? Do you look for evidence that the way you've always seen it is right, or are you open to learning or embracing something new?

Attitude to Risk: There's just no getting away from it, being self-employed is inherently riskier than working for someone else. There's no organisation or structure behind you to catch you when you fall. If you get it wrong, it's on you, and only you. Learning to manage risk is an important skill when you're self-employed.

Risks come in many shapes and sizes but to name just a few: there's no social welfare or company illness scheme to cover your income if you get sick; no one steps in to look after your clients when you go on holidays; there's no finance department to take care of the bookkeeping and bill paying; if a client sues you, it's you who will be turning up in court and paying the bill.

When you work for someone else, these issues will be covered by the structure of the organisation, so while there may still be fallout if something goes wrong, the company net will generally be there to catch you.

There are ways to manage these risks. How you choose to relate to them depends on your attitude. The first step is to come to terms with the reality that risk is there, and it can't be avoided. But you can put in place checks and balances that can support you. You can plan your activities so that all the risk does not land at the same time. For example, you can ease your way out of an employment position, by going part time, or starting to see clients at night time, rather than going cold turkey and leaving the day job before you have another stream of income. You can manage the risk of being left without an income by creating more than one income source, or accumulating a nest egg of money in case you are unable to work for some time. You can structure your practice and professional life in such a way that there are others around to support you.

To help you better understand your own attitude to risk, play around with situations that you find edgy. Say something out loud that you might otherwise keep back. Put €10 on a horse. Be willing to make mistakes, and explore what happens to you when you do. Do you criticise yourself for failing, or do you appreciate yourself for trying? Do you give up at the first hurdle?

Embracing Uncertainty: In many ways, therapists are good with uncertainty; learning to sit with the discomfort of not knowing is an integral part of most therapy training. However, outside the therapy room can be a different question. Some of the uncertainty encountered as a self-employed person relates to the flow of work and consequently of money. An employee knows with reasonable certainty that their salary will be paid weekly or monthly by their employer. They know the amount of the salary, the day it will be paid, and that tax at the appropriate rate will be deducted.

A self-employed person has no such certainty. The flow of income can fluctuate from day to day and week to week. Clients who have previously been predictable and reliable attendees and payers can suddenly disappear, taking that stream of income with them. Seasonal fluctuations are common.

To help you become more comfortable with taking financial risks, familiarise yourself with basic financial planning tools. Learn to record and be aware of your money. Make plans and budgets, and use them to support your uncertainty, by leaving some room for changing circumstances. In relation to all risks, recognise that they exist, and learn what helps and supports you, and do more of that.

Patience and Compassion: Last but not least, these two attributes will stand to you when things get difficult. It would be great if everything worked out right first time we tried it, but that is often not the way. Understand that building a practice is a process, and takes time. Remember the law of the harvest. And be gentle with yourself through the early stages, as you begin to find your feet.

Having Confidence In Yourself

I often hear from practitioners that they feel a lack of confidence around the business side of their practice. Any of you who have ever learned a new skill will know that confidence comes with repetition. Maybe that's why it's called a practice!

Practising the skills I talk about above will help to strengthen your confidence in yourself. And don't forget to acknowledge and celebrate your successes, even the tiny ones. You will find your practice thriving.

Mix with others who are at the same stage as yourself. Share experiences, triumphs and tribulations. If there is an area of managing or running your practice that fills you with dread, maybe you could support yourself by doing some training in that area? Or asking someone who has already done it for their secret?

Learn to trust yourself more by noticing and celebrating small successes and wins.

It's A Relationship

If your practice were an object, what would it be?

It's hard for most of us to see ourselves as separate from our practices, especially if the practice is just us! But an ability to see the practice as a separate entity really helps us when it comes to taking ownership. It helps us to think more clearly about it, and about what we might need to do.

It's tempting to see our practice as our clients, and their needs, but this misses the important piece about our own needs, and the needs of the practice, and how those needs will be satisfied.

Your practice is not you, even though you are an integral part of it. It has an identity that is heavily influenced by who you are, but is not the same as you. For example, there will inevitably be parts of your life that you will not wish to share with your clients, or to be known by the general public. You may choose to adopt certain policies for the sake of the work which acknowledge that you are adopting a role.

It is helpful to explore this concept of being in relationship with your practice. How do you feel about being responsible for your practice? How do you feel about some of the tasks that go along with being self-employed that might push you far beyond your comfort or familiar zone? What do you expect from your practice? And what are you willing to contribute? If you and your practice were entering into a prenuptial agreement, what is on the table, and what is out of bounds? Are you willing to learn, to grow and to stretch in this relationship? What support do you need from your practice? And what supports can you offer your practice?

Conclusion

When you trained to become a counsellor or therapist, there were certain things you had to learn and unlearn. Perhaps you had a desire to rescue clients, or to give advice, and had to learn instead to sit back and tolerate your own and your clients' discomfort. Perhaps you found it difficult to be assertive and had to learn to stand your ground in certain situations. You might never have had to grow in these ways if you weren't training to be a counsellor or therapist.

In a similar way, there are skills that you will need to learn in order to run your own practice, however small it might be. In the same way that having a house plant or a car demands certain things of you, so too does being a business owner. And these are not the same skills and experiences that you need to do the client work.

Taking ownership of your practice is about acknowledging that running your own business requires you to be in relationship with your practice, and to own the responsibilities and challenges of that.

Exercise: Reflection

Read back over the Attributes of Business Ownership above and see which resonate most strongly with you. Which attributes do you feel you already have, and which do you need to develop? Below, note the three attributes you'd most like to focus on and choose one small action you could take to stretch yourself in this area:

Attributes I'd like to develop and related actions I will take:

Attribute 1:

Action I will take:

Attribute 2:

Action I will take:

Attribute 3:

Action I will take:

Part 5:

The Second Pillar: Knowing Your Practice

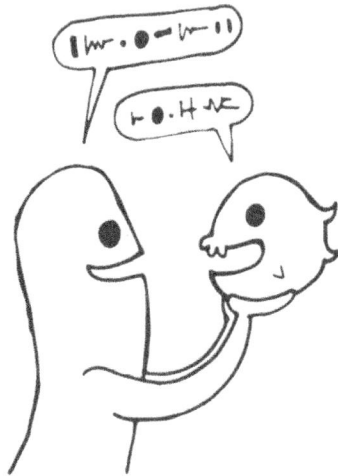

KNOWING

"Knowing yourself is the beginning of all wisdom"[5]

> **Goals:** Identity, vision
>
> **Key tasks:** Creating a business plan
>
> **Key mindset:** Willingness to make choices and decisions

In this chapter we're going to look at the second pillar of a successful practice, Knowing Your Practice. Initially, this will mean getting to know the basic building blocks you need to put in place, what you are going to call your practice, where you are going to practise from, and what shape your practice might take. However, this pillar continues to have relevance throughout your practising career as you hone your preferences, and sort out what works for you and what doesn't.

The goals of this pillar are identity and vision. By getting some clarity about the identity of your practice and a picture of what you'd like it to look like, the steps you need to take become easier to identify. The mindset needed to create this picture is one of being willing to make decisions and choices, to sift and sort through your options to focus on what's right for you. To move from the conceptual to the practical, you need to make choices about what your practice will look and feel like. The structure or task that you will use to do this is to create a business plan.

A Business Plan For Your Therapy Practice

A business plan is a key tool in defining the shape of the

practice you want to create. A business plan is a plan for your business. Organisations of every size have a plan, though often they may not be committed to paper, or communicated to employees in a way that makes sense. Regardless of the size of the business, a business plan keeps the focus on what's important and where the business is going. A huge global corporation will have a long, detailed plan covering every aspect of their business, but for a small professional practice, it's a much shorter and simpler affair.

Many small businesses don't take the trouble to create a business plan until they need one to apply for finance with their bank. But a business plan is much more than just a document to satisfy bank requirements. Even if you have no intention of borrowing money, a business plan will repay many times over the time and effort it takes to prepare it.

A lot of the introductory sections of a business plan are filled with straightforward factual information, such as what your practice will be called, and where it will be based, how you can be contacted, legal status (sole practice, partnership, company), details of financial and legal advisors and principal staff (if any). Many of these details will already be known to you, some may not. If not, this is an opportunity to start thinking about them.

However, the real value of the business plan, and where you will most benefit from taking time to think about it, is deciding your preferences under the following headings:

1. **Values, Vision, Purpose:** What is driving you to set up in practice? What is important to you in the work? What do you hope your practice will achieve for those you serve?

2. **Strengths and weaknesses of your practice:** What are the gifts you bring to this work? What skills and expertise do you have? What defences or struggles do you bring that might sabotage you?

3. **Desired environment:** Town or country? Alone or with others? Traditional or alternative? Spiritual or practical? Energetic or serene? Who are you going to be competing with? Which existing service most closely matches yours, or are you going for something that's completely new?

4. **Your offering:** What are you going to offer? What services are you going to provide? Who are you going to provide them to? Who are you most drawn to working with, what are their problems, their challenges, their desires? In what way are you hoping your services will benefit those who come to you for help? How are you going to reach them? (We will cover this issue in greater detail in Part 6: The Third Pillar: Growing Your Practice.)

5. **Risks:** What do you perceive as the business risks? What could go wrong, where might your practice be vulnerable? How do you intend to respond to those risks?

6. **Financial Information:** Create a detailed budget and

cash flow for the early years, a more general one for future years, and historical income and expenditure details if you have them.

You may never need to share your business plan with anyone, or to use it to borrow money for your practice, but getting clear about your ideas now, before you get going, will support you in ways you can't imagine now. Time spent now on these issues will help you to grow more confidence about who you want to be in your practice going forward. It will help you to focus your marketing activities, and it will help you to identify potential problems and take action to avoid them before those problems have actually landed in your lap! When you're in doubt and don't know how to move forward, your business plan brings you back to the road you have laid out for yourself. In other words, it puts you into the driving seat of your practice.

It will also help you avoid wasting time, energy and money on strategies you later realise were not right for you.

My website has a simple example of how a business plan for a small therapy practice might look. You can find it at http://tinyurl.com/jpcjwa6

You might want to start with an outline of a business plan, and as we go through this book make notes as ideas occur to you. Later, you can go back to your notes and see how they now look in light of all you've read. You may wish to revisit some aspects of the business plan at that stage. Finally, you can use your business plan to give you the steps you need to take to implement what you've decided.

At the end of this chapter, I'll give you an exercise to help you start creating your own business plan.

Should I Work For Myself Or For Someone Else?

Not everyone who trains to be a therapist does so with the intention of setting up their own practice. Some train because it will supplement their core training or because they intend to use the skills in their current occupation.

The question of whether you want to work for yourself or for someone else is an important one because the skill set needed to be self-employed is different from that needed to be an employee. If you haven't ever worked for yourself and have always been employed, this may not be self-evident. Whether they know it or not, most people will have a tendency towards one choice rather than the other. This tendency is informed by (among other things) their own work experiences and the experiences of their upbringing. Neither is right or wrong; like many of these issues, it's a question of personal preference.

At its most basic, working for someone else involves a willingness and ability to work within parameters set by your employer, whereas working for yourself means having the ability and willingness to set those parameters for yourself.

Working for Yourself

There are many reasons why people choose to be self-employed. The main ones are:

- Income: Wanting to determine their own level of income

- Independence and control: Wanting to be independent of the requirements of other people and have control over all aspects of their work

- Flexibility to suit themselves: Wanting flexibility to choose when, where, and how they work

- Challenge: Wanting the satisfaction that comes from rising to the challenge of being self-employed

- Social responsibility: Meeting the desire to make a difference in the world, and give something back

Some may choose to be self-employed because they believe they cannot get what they want from employment.

The Best Of Both Worlds

Some people choose to do both, working part time for an agency or employer, and part-time self-employed in private practice. This allows you to have both the security of being employed and the freedom of private practice at the same time. If this is your intention, don't forget to check the terms of your employment first. You won't want to risk doing something which is prohibited.

Comparison Of Advantages And Disadvantages Of Being Self-Employed And An Employee

The main differences between being an employee and self-employed are summarised in the following table.

Self-Employed	Employee
Freedom to choose and make the rules: who you work with and when, what you charge, where you work, what hours you keep, what policies you apply.	**These matters are generally decided by your employer.** Your employer will dictate your working hours, what and how many clients you see, where you work and the policies that govern your workplace.
Responsibilities: It is your job to make sure there is enough work. All the other chores such as cleaning, bookkeeping, paying bills, putting insurance in place, submitting tax returns etc. are all your responsibility.	**These matters are generally the responsibility of your employer.** Your employer is responsible for creating a safe working environment and for ensuring housekeeping and all other tasks are done. In Ireland, it is the responsibility of the employer to deduct and return income tax from salaries.

Risks: If there isn't enough work, your income suffers. If you don't have enough money in the bank, the bills won't get paid. When you are sick or on holidays, there is no pay cheque. If a client sues, they'll be suing you.	**Risks** are carried by your employer. You will usually be paid when you are sick or on holidays. It is your employer's job to make sure there is enough money to pay your salary. If a client sues you, it is the employer who faces the challenge.
Supports: You decide what you need in the way of training and supervision. You get to choose them, and you also have to pay for them, and find the time for them. There is no organisation to support you, so you will have to create support for yourself to prevent isolation.	**Supports:** Your employer decides what supports they are willing to provide. Your employer may pay for them, or provide them within your working day. Also, you have the benefit of the support of the structure of the organisation, colleagues, managers, etc.
Rewards: If work is plentiful, you reap the financial rewards. You decide how much to charge, and how much your time is worth.	**Rewards:** Your financial rewards are decided by your employer, and if money is plentiful, your employer reaps the benefits.
Job security: There is no job security. You have no employment rights when you are self-employed.	**Job security:** You are entitled to the security provided by your contract of employment, together with the rights afforded by employment law.
Structure: You decide and provide such structure as you require. You provide the organisation for yourself.	**Structure:** Your employer decides what structure and organisation is needed.

Home or Away: Where to Set Up Your Practice

Often, the question of where to establish your practice comes down to practicalities of costs and convenience. I would encourage you to begin by asking yourself what is your vision for the long term; not what you think you can achieve, but what you'd really like if there were no restrictions. In life, too often we can settle for what we think we deserve, or what we believe we can possibly get. We are limited in our thinking to what we have experienced in the past or what others have told us is possible. Start by imagining what you would really like. You may not be able to achieve it on day one, but knowing where you want to go helps to determine the route you take.

There are advantages and disadvantages to both working at home and elsewhere. There is no right or wrong answer other than the one that fits best for you.

Working from Home

If you have space, working from home is convenient and there are some obvious advantages. There won't be any rent to pay, and no additional costs of buying or upkeep of the premises; you may have suitable furniture in your home that you can use. As the place is your own you can furnish it as you wish, without having to consider the views of others. If you have a room that is underused or not used at all, this may be a good option for you. It will be familiar, and that familiarity may offer you some support and comfort. You can be more flexible about cancellations or changes in appointments since your time can be easily used elsewhere in the home.

Does this seem like a no-brainer? Perhaps.

The other side is that it is your home.

The most important thing for you to consider is how you will feel about the loss of your privacy. Clients will be coming into your home and your space, rather than into a more neutral, anonymous one. You may be okay with this or you may not.

Consider the following questions:

- How do you feel about clients knowing where you live?
- Do you like to keep a clear division between your home life and your work life?
- How do you manage a client's curiosity about you?
- Do you find it easy to keep your home clean and clutter free?
- Will sounds of family or pets be an issue?
- Is the room you are thinking of using close to the entrance?
- Is there a bathroom close by?
- Are you sensitive to the energy of others?
- Are you comfortable working with distressed or angry clients within your home?
- Will the room be used only for your therapy work? If not, how do you feel about having personal items in the

room when a client is there?

- Is there parking close by that will not inconvenience neighbours?

- Is there somewhere for clients to wait if they are early, or if you are running late?

- How will you manage callers to the door during sessions?

Some years ago, I visited a therapist who worked from their home. The therapy room was a small spare room which was accessed through a separate entrance at the side of the house. I was led through the therapist's utility room, which was piled high with domestic appliances, sports equipment, airing clothes, pet food dishes and so on. I found myself being really curious looking around me as I passed through. But I also felt as if I was intruding on her personal space. If you're going to invite clients into your house, you might want to ask a colleague or a friend how it might appear if they were a client.

While working from your home can bring more flexibility, it can also work against you if you have a tendency to overwork. The discipline of having to travel to work and pay rent imposes a structure and boundary that helps to limit the time you spend at work.

You probably won't want to hang a sign outside the front door of your home, or put signs on the windows advertising your service, so you may have to work a bit harder to achieve visibility than you would if you were practising from premises in the centre of town. When a therapist first sets up in practice, they may imagine that once they qualify (or get accreditation), the clients will just flow in. It doesn't really work like that for most people. This is especially true if you choose to work from home.

Check out with your accountant, local authority, landlord or property management company whether you are legally entitled to run a business from your home. If you own your own home, there may be tax or other consequences of changing the use from a residential premises to a business one (even if it's only a partial change of use.) You may be able to claim some of your household expenses against your income for tax purposes, but making such a claim may backfire in other ways by firmly establishing that you are running a business from your home. And you can't claim ALL the expenses of your home, only a proportion.

Working Outside The Home

Depending on where and what you choose, working outside the home may mean renting a room which is exclusively for your own use, or sharing space with others. Each has its advantages and disadvantages.

Renting a space which is used by you alone has the advantage that you can make it your own. You can arrange it as you wish, and the articles or decoration in the room will be for you to decide. The energy will be that of you and your clients, and be unaffected by others. You can use it when you wish without reference to the needs or timetables of others. However, unless you are seeing a lot of clients, this may turn out to be an expensive option, as you will have to pay for the room even when you are not using it. If you decide to go this way, check with your lease whether you can rent the unused time on to others, to help meet the costs.

Another option is sharing space with others, whether it's a single room used for the purpose or as part of a centre where therapy or related services are provided. One advantage of this choice is this that renting on an hourly or block basis is likely to cost less than renting a dedicated space. A block basis means you rent it for a particular day or portion of a day and you pay for the time whether or not you see clients.

When sharing space in a therapy or counselling centre, there may be potential for referrals from the centre, which may or may not attract a referral fee. In a centre that is used for different services, such as an holistic centre or medical practice, there may also be the potential for referrals from other service providers in the premises. You will need to network with them so they understand and appreciate the services you provide and how they can complement theirs.

The option of sharing a space may give you the bonus of having contact with others. The work can be solitary, and personally I get a lot from the support, camaraderie and friendship of my colleagues where I practice.

The disadvantage of sharing space is that you do just that: you share a space. You may not have control over the appearance or decoration of the room. You may have less flexibility about the timing of bookings. The room may not always be available when you want it to be and you have to rely on those who use the space immediately before you to finish up on time, and leave the room tidy. You may have limited control over the temperature of the room or over the noise from the surrounding rooms.

Since I first started in practice, I have chosen to work in a shared space. Currently, I work from two counselling centres, where other therapists use the space as well. I have also worked from a dedicated room in a doctor's surgery and I have seen some clients in their own homes. All of these options have worked well for me.

Summary Comparison of Pros and Cons of Working from Your Home versus Working in an Outside Premises

Home	Away
Cost effective but potential tax or other consequences	You will incur rental and other costs
Greater freedom over the layout and contents of room	There may be some restriction in the layout of the room
Control over availability of room	Availability of room may be subject to negotiation with others
Good use of unused/underused space	A dedicated therapy space
Familiarity of home environment	Neutral environment
Flexibility of reassigning your time in event of client cancellation	A late cancellation may mean lost time or rental cost
Possible loss of privacy; managing clients' curiosity; safety issues with some clients	Anonymity of space; safety issues with some clients
Need to keep quiet, free from clutter and personal belongings	Dedicated therapy space; art materials or other items can be left between sessions
Less separation between work and home; need to manage boundaries and clear energy to reclaim space	Clear separation between work and home
Potential for isolation from other therapists	Potential for interaction with other therapists
Need for client parking	Need for personal and client parking
Less publicly visible	More publicly visible
Need for nearby bathroom facilities	Bathroom facilities present

Working By Yourself Or With Others?

Should you work on your own or with others? Is it better to practise as an individual or in partnership or association with others? A lot comes down to personal preference, and therapists vary hugely. The following questions may help you with this:

- Do you work better on your own or with others?

- Do you find it hard to stick to a time schedule?

- How do you feel about knowing that someone else needs the room shortly after a session ends?

- Do you use "props" in your work, such as art materials, books, figurines, etc?

- How do you feel about your belongings being moved, or having to move them at the end of a session?

- How sensitive are you to changes in your work environment?

- Do you prefer to work within an organisation where the tasks may be shared and the provision of services is available?

- Or do you prefer to go it alone, with the freedom that that can bring?

- Would you prefer to know that your space is available for you whenever you want to use it?

- Or would you prefer to keep costs to a minimum by

only paying for the hours for which you know you are going to use the room?

I found it to be hugely beneficial to me to have my colleague Jennifer working alongside me and sharing the tasks of setting up. When we were trying to find premises to work from, it was really helpful to have someone else to go along and look at the rooms with me, to talk to the people we met, and to compare notes with afterwards. Jennifer would focus on different aspects than I, and it helped that our visions and desires were similar enough that we could pick somewhere that suited both of us but dissimilar enough to bring a broader perspective to the discussion.

One Last Word …

If you are thinking of working with someone else, be aware there are legal and tax issues involved where a partnership exists, so you need to be clear about whether you do or do not intend your association with another practitioner to be a partnership.

A partnership is a separate legal entity, and if a partnership exists, each partner is jointly and severally liable for the debts of the partnership, which means you may be liable for a share of debt greater than the share of the business you own. You can read more about your choices for structuring your practice in Part 7: How To Structure Your Therapy Practice.

What's In a Name?

A name is important. And deciding what to call your practice is an important part of the process of establishing yourself as a self-employed practitioner. There are so many things to think about. Should you use your own name? Or should you opt for something that conjures up an image in your mind or the minds of potential clients? Should you choose something that conveys the essence of the practice you're hoping to create? Here are some things you might like to think about when deciding what your business is going to be called:

- **Choose something that will last:** Unless this is a once-off type of project (in which case you'd be better picking something really specific to this project), you'll probably want the name to be something that you'll be able to use for the foreseeable future. So if, for example, the name includes a date or address, and then something changes, the name will no longer fit so well. "New Millennium Counselling" may have captured the spirit of 1999, but seems a bit dated in 2016. "Ballybunion Therapy Centre" is ideal as long as you stay in Ballybunion, but may not be appropriate if you open a branch in Dingle.

- **Choose a name that describes what you do:** If you are planning to work with a specific issue, consider choosing a name that makes that clear. Kildare Bereavement

Counselling or Couples Therapy Centre lets people know what you do. You might also use your speciality or philosophy as a tagline, in the same way that Ryanair used the tag, "The Low Fares Airline."

- **Don't exclude potential clients by being too obtuse:** Unless you want to appeal only to those who fit a narrow set of criteria, be careful of using another language or an obscure reference only understood by the initiated. This may include the approach you use, unless it is widely understood. You run the risk of turning potential clients away.

- **Don't make it complicated:** If someone wants to pass your name to a friend, it helps if it's easily spelt and pronounced.

- **People may assume the name reflects your name:** I learned this one the hard way! I'm often asked, "Can I speak to Anne Leigh?" I then have to explain that AnneLeigh is the business name and that my name is Jude.

- **Before making your final choice:** Check it out on the Internet and with the Companies Registration Office, to see if there's another business with the same name. It's also a good idea if you're planning to have a website to check out the available domain names, as you'll want to get one that is close to your business name. Even if you're not yet ready to set up a website, consider buying the domain name now. It doesn't cost much and ensures you get what you want.

- **Did You Know?** If you trade under a business name that differs in any way from your own true surname, you must register the business name with the Companies Registration Office. What is your own true surname? The CRO advise that registration is required if:

  "an individual uses a business name which differs in any way from his/her true surname. It makes no difference whether the individual's first name or initials are added. So registration is required if, for example, Mr. John Murphy traded as Murphy Builders but not if he traded as Murphy or John Murphy."

If you choose to have a .ie domain name for your website and you aren't calling your practice by your own true surname (e.g., judefaycounselling.ie,) you will have to register the business name with CRO before you can claim your .ie domain name.

See https://www.cro.ie/Registration/Business-Name or http://tinyurl.com/grd9j7x for more details, or go to https://www.cro.ie/en-ie/Help/Using-CORE/Registering-a-Business-Name-Online or http://tinyurl.com/hf7axoz to register your business name online.

Exercise: Start to Create a Business Plan for Your Practice

Note: You will not be able to complete all of this plan at once, so don't be too hard on yourself. These headings are not a test you have to pass, but a framework to help you begin to form a vision of the type of practice you'd like to have. Read through it, and jot down notes where you already have ideas. You can come back to it again and again as you read through the chapters in this book.

Practice Business Plan

1. **Name:** My practice is going to be called...

2. **Location:** My practice is going to be based...

3. **Structure:** My practice is going to be...

4. **Values, Vision, Purpose:** I am setting up this practice because I am passionate about...The values that support my practice are... It is important to me that clients of my practice will benefit from working with me in the following ways...

5. **Strengths and Weaknesses of my Practice:** Clients will come to me because... They will pay for my services because... I bring these personal qualities to the work? I have had these experiences...and acquired these skills and expertise... I can sabotage myself by...

6. **Desired Environment:** My practice will be based... These words best fit the environment I'd like to operate from...

7. **Competition:** My main competitors are... These existing service most closely match mine... My offering is different from my peers in that...

8. **My Offering:** I am going to offer these services...

9. **My Clients:** I am going to provide my services to... I am most drawn to working with... Their problems are... Their challenges are... Their desires are... My services will benefit them in these ways...

10. **Marketing:** These factors are unique to me and my practice... I see my clients as coming to me through the following channels... I am going to reach these clients to let them know I am available to help them by...

11. **My Time Contribution:** I have this much time available to work with clients (per week, month year)... I am also willing to spend this much time to work on developing my practice (per week, month)...

12. **Fees and duration:** My clients will be willing to pay me this much... They will pay me this because... Clients will continue to come and see me for...(weeks, sessions, months, years)

13. **Costs:** It will cost me €... to see clients (per hour,

week, month)

14. **Risks:** These are the business risks I will be facing...My practice could be vulnerable in these ways... I intend to respond to those risks by...

15. **Viability:** My therapy practice will be viable because...

16. **Financial Information:** I want to earn € after costs, each (week, month, year)...

Part 6:

The Third Pillar: Growing Your Practice

GROWING

"If we are growing we are always going to be outside our comfort zone."[6]

Goals: Survival, longevity and prosperity

Key tasks: Getting out there

Key mindset: Willingness to be seen

Having found a place to practice and started to put the framework in place, you'll want to get some clients. This process will be much easier for you if you have an idea of what you'd like your practice to look like. Before we go on, take a moment to look back to the exercise we completed earlier, where you looked at your vision for your practice, and at the outline of the business plan we started to create. You may have some questions at this stage. Note them down now, so that we can begin to answer them as we go through this section.

The goal of this section is to help you establish a flow of work. This is essential to your long-term survival as a therapist. Clients do not stay forever, so a constant flow of work is needed to ensure a steady income. The greatest obstacle to achieving a steady flow of work is not the market, the availability of clients or their willingness to pay, or any other external factor. The biggest obstacle to attracting clients is your willingness to take the action necessary to bring clients to your door. And this is in large part dictated by your willingness to be seen.

This is a difficult one for many therapists, as we can be an introverted lot! If putting yourself out there is something that you think may be a challenge for you, you might like to see my EFT video[7] on this subject: Being Seen. You'll find it at https://youtu.be/OUJ0VcWnshQ

The Inner Reality Reflected In The Outer

The process of carrying out some of the tasks, such as preparing promotional material or developing a web presence, may seem daunting, especially if you are new to that sort of thing. However, they are worth doing. Even if you do not get one new client from it, working with and clearing your resistance to taking these steps has benefits which will stand to you in the work. You are creating an image of yourself in your practice and, over time, the external reality will reflect your inner vision.

To put it another way, you can look at the tasks of getting business cards or brochures or setting up a website as the external reflection of how you see yourself as a therapist. If you are struggling with getting started on these tasks, perhaps you are also struggling with the concept of what it means to you to be a therapist. Do you feel able, qualified and ready? If you are finding it hard to say what you have to offer a client, perhaps you are not clear or confident that you do have something to offer? If you are concerned about the exposure of putting your contact details out into the world, perhaps some part of you is fearful that clients will come?

So, before running off to start promoting your services, take a little time to reflect on what you have to offer a potential client.

This will stand to you down the road because it is possible to waste a lot of time and money putting yourself out there with little or no return.

How Do I Decide How To Promote My Practice?

What attracts a client to one professional rather than to another? It is hard to say categorically that *this* is the right or best thing to do to attract clients or *this* will work for all therapists setting out for the first time. Some potential clients will focus on a personal recommendation or the recommendation of another professional such as a doctor. Some people focus on anonymity, some on the convenience and location, some will decide on a whim. Some will be drawn to the wording of an advertisement; some will be put off by the same wording. Some will like a logo or sign, while others will dislike it. Some will focus on the price of your service.

Bear in mind, a prospective client may see your name or the name of your practice several times when they have no need of your services. When the need arises, if your name is familiar to them, because they have seen or heard of you before, it may influence them to approach you rather another practitioner. So don't underestimate the power of just having your name out there, even if it's hard to translate it directly into numbers in your rooms.

Whatever route you choose, make sure it feels authentic and congruent for you. Satisfy yourself that you are attracted to it, have an emotional connection with it and that it is congruent with your values and beliefs. Don't try to second-guess what prospective clients might think, you can't know, and they are as many as they are varied. That is not to say that you cannot and should not listen to others' views. Take advice by all means, but don't necessarily rely on what someone else says. Hold on to your own inner voice of, "This is right for me." By doing what helps you to feel supported within yourself, you are most likely to attract clients that are a good fit for you.

What Do You Have To Offer?

According to Anthony Storr, the average therapist (insofar as there is such a thing) is more likely to be introverted, self-effacing, and inclined to put others' needs before their own.[8] It can be a difficult task for anyone to set out their strengths and what they bring to the work. However, to promote your practice, you need to have some idea of what you are bringing to a client. It will be different for everyone. Here are some ideas to get you started:

If a client were to describe how you interact with them in the work, what would they be likely to say? Do you bring ...

- Interest
- Commitment
- Empathy
- Relationship
- Holding and accompaniment

- Specialist knowledge, training and accreditation
- Skill
- Time
- Availability

Do you know how rare it is for many of those who attend as clients to receive these gifts? Or how you uniquely bring each of these qualities (and perhaps others that aren't listed here) to your client work? Do you appreciate the gift that you are to your clients? Add your own special gifts to the list above as they come to mind.

What Is My Product?

So, having thought a little about what you personally bring to the work, in what shape are you going to bring that to your clients?

Are you planning to do traditional therapy sessions with clients? If so, who are your clients going to be?

- Are you going to work one-to-one, with couples, families, or groups?
- Will you work with children, teens or elders?
- Are you going to work face-to-face or are you thinking about providing your services through email, by phone, or Skype (or similar)?
- Do you have a preference for the length of contract?

Are you thinking short term or long term? Fixed contract or open-ended contract?

- Are you going to provide counselling or psychotherapy?

- What approach are you going to use?

- What issues do you see yourself working with?

You don't have to have answers to all these questions when you initially set out, but any that you can answer immediately will help you to shape the way you promote your practice. For example, if you are planning to provide email or Skype services, you may move more towards an online approach to promotion. We'll talk more about these issues later in this chapter.

How Do I Go About Getting Clients?

Unless you work for an organisation which refers clients to you, you are going to have to find clients for yourself. For most practitioners, this is an ongoing process throughout their professional careers, though with luck, as you become more established and create a reputation for yourself, it will take less work.

So where do clients come from? There are many sources of clients, but the main ones are:

- Self-referrals

- Doctors and health professional referrals

- Referrals from other therapists

- Referrals from former or existing clients.

To connect with these people, you will need to market your practice. If you have never had any experience of marketing, or find the idea of putting yourself out there abhorrent, you may need to get some help with this aspect of establishing your practice. Unfortunately, being good at what you do isn't enough to bring clients to your door, you also need to be visible enough for potential clients to find you. I'm going to start by looking at who you are hoping your clients will be, and what services you are going to provide.

Remember, "if you're marketing to everyone, you're marketing to no-one." So it's important to get some clarity about who you are going to be marketing your services to. That's why it's good to start this process by identifying what services you are going to provide. If you haven't done the exercises above to identify what you're offering, go back and do it now.

Let's say for example that you know you want to work with children. You can use that knowledge to guide how and where you market your services. Where might you find parents, guardians, or teachers of children in difficulty? You might try schools, support groups for parents, or online chat groups about parenting. If you have young children of your own, you might talk to parents at the school gates, in sports or other activities where children and parents are to be found. The same principle applies for any other work. Where you want to get to determines the direction you'll choose.

Sometimes therapists say to me that they don't want to get too specific about the type of work they want to attract as they might end up being pigeonholed. This is not true in my experience. Those who have very specialised practices will often work with other issues. Also, although some clients may present with very finely defined issues, the work often spreads into other areas.

One very good reason for narrowing the scope of your work is because it will make your marketing easier in so many ways. For a start, you will be more focused in your ideas and your language, and you will recognise what you want more easily as it fits into the vision you have created for yourself.

When I first qualified as a therapist, I found it hard to believe that I'd ever have more work than I needed, so I was willing to work with any client on any issue. As time has gone on, and I have become more relaxed about the whole thing, I have grown in confidence that there are plenty of clients out there. The trick then is *how do I get them to come to me? How can I help clients to find me?*

Help Clients to Find You by Thinking Like Them

A common mistake that therapists make in promoting their practices is to assume that because they decide to go into practice that clients will find them. They think that because they feel very exposed when they promote themselves, and because they may fear that clients might see their marketing as pushy, that they are in fact exposed, or they are pushy. The opposite is more likely to be true. As a result, many therapists may be overly limiting their promotional efforts, and then feeling disappointed when they yield little results.

Potential clients are swamped with information. Personally, I have to spend time each week keeping on top of my inbox, and the hundreds of emails I receive. And that's just one medium. There's also the Internet, newspapers, television and radio, regular post, flyers, brochures, magazines, and word of mouth. To find the service they need, potential clients have to navigate through all the available options to arrive at one that's right for them. So a single ad, a single flyer, or a single post on a blog or social media website is likely to be lost.

Speaking with a group of newly qualified therapists one day, we brainstormed the different ways in which they had found their own therapists. There was a chorus of comments such as "Oh, I never thought of that!" as a whole range of routes emerged. Although each of them had sought out their own therapist in a particular way, most never made the connection that they could reverse that route, and use it as a means of finding clients.

One way to think about helping clients to find you is to ask yourself, "If I were looking for a therapist, what would I do?" Let's say I want to find a therapist who can help my daughter to get over her recent relationship break-up. Where would I start? I could ...

- Ask a friend, relative or GP for a recommendation

- Research it on the Internet

- Consult a professional body

- Look at a phone book

- Walk around the locality looking at door and window signage

- Consult an employee assistance programme, if I have access to one

- Consult a local paper, magazine or directory for an advertisement

Each of the options set out in the bullets above is a possible source of referral for you too. How many of them are you using? Going to see a counsellor or therapist is a big step for anyone, even if they know they need it. It's difficult to make that first move so help your potential client to find you.

Unique Selling Point

In deciding on how best to describe you and your practice, it's helpful to think about what differentiates you from other practitioners who may be providing what appears to be the same service. This is known in the business world as your Unique Selling Point or USP.

Your USP may be your own personal story, to which others may relate (e.g., that you work with families bereaved by suicide, because you have some experience of that). You may have a particular training or qualification that others don't. It may be that your values or beliefs or your love of animals or poetry or art bring a particular quality to your work. It may be that you speak more than one language. It may be the way you approach your work or the particular locality you practice from. It may be the quality of the presence you bring to your client or the atmosphere of your therapy room.

Find something that distinguishes you and use it to tell your prospective clients something about you. You may refer to it directly in the language you use, or indirectly through images, colours or photos. If you find this difficult, ask friends and family to give you three words that they would use to describe you to someone you'd never met before. Ask them to say what they most like about you. Or ask a colleague or supervisor who has worked with you, or is familiar with your work, what they would say about you.

Clients begin to form a relationship with you from the first point of contact, when they see or hear your name or photo. This may be long before they call to make an appointment. What would you like them to know?

One accountant I knew solved this problem by getting himself known for having an unusual talent. You can read about him on my website at http://thisbusinessoftherapy.com/and-then-there-was-the-accountant-who-spun-plates/ or http://tinyurl.com/hhdsxxg While his solution may be a bit over the top for you, the point is worth considering. For those who have never made themselves visible before, it's a common fear that everyone else will be as focused on what you say or do as you are. Actually, the opposite is more often true. There are so many choices out there that you have to shout quite loudly to be heard.

Until you have established a reputation, you may have to work quite hard to get those first few clients. So if your first efforts don't give you the rewards you expected, don't get too disappointed! It takes time to build some momentum, and to smooth out the bumps along the way. Be prepared to keep promoting your practice with no visible sign of return for a while. Remember, a client may be thinking about coming to therapy for a while before they pick up the phone or send you a message. Give your efforts time to bear fruit.

Sources Of Referrals

It's important to think widely about who might refer clients to you. Many therapists think solely of doctors, and while GPs and other health professionals can certainly be a good source of work, there are many potential clients who will not think of their doctor when faced with a problem.

Anyone you know is a potential source of referral for you. This includes:

- Friends and neighbours
- Family
- Past or present work colleagues

- Past or present tutors

- Other counsellors or psychotherapists, and

- Any professionals in a caring or health-related field.

To learn more about this issue, visit my website at thisbusinessoftherapy.com to get your free copy of my report "Five Ways to Boost Your Therapy Practice" at http://tinyurl.com/h3xv49r

Referrals come from many sources. If like me you work in a therapy centre, some referrals may come to you directly through that route. They may also come from

- Doctors

- Other health professionals (physiotherapists, chiropractors, dentists, etc.)

- Your own website

- Internet directories (paid and unpaid)

- Former or existing clients.

Note: In some cases, boundary issues may prevent you seeing potential clients where another relationship already exists. However, in this situation, you can refer them on to a colleague, who hopefully will reciprocate when the opportunity arises.

It is useful to ask a new client where they got your name as this will help you to keep track of what promotional activity is working for you.

What works for one therapist may not work for another, and what works this week may not work next week. So keep an open mind about your promotional activities. You need to have more than one source of work. I'll talk a bit more about each of these ways below.

It's not always possible to predict where you will get your work from. It is my personal belief that it is important to put some energy into generating work, particularly in the early days. However, where you invest your energy may not be where the work comes from. Willingness to put some energy into the promotion of your practice can bring rewards in ways we cannot anticipate. In opening ourselves to approaches that are unfamiliar or even uncomfortable for us, we meet the resistance that is getting in the way of allowing more in. We become more aware of where *we* are creating the obstacles (and can do something about it), rather than focusing on those obstacles that are outside of ourselves in the environment (where there's little we can do about it.)

To put it another way, I may need to grow to be ready for the new work I say I want. This is one of the reasons why I stress the importance of continuing to work on yourself.

Choosing A Niche Or Target Market

A niche market is where you are aiming to work with a particular sector of the population. It may be defined by the presenting issue (see my comments on specialisation below) or by some characteristics that your clients have in common.

For example, in the broad category of bereavement counselling, bereaved relatives of suicides is a niche market, as is bereaved spouses or children. In the area of addiction counselling, eating disorders is a niche market.

From a marketing perspective, the idea of having a niche market is that you are focusing your efforts towards a specific portion of the overall population, and it can save you time and effort promoting to those who are unlikely to want to avail of your services.

Having a niche also helps those who might refer work to you. A doctor who is seeing a patient with an eating disorder, for example, may feel more comfortable referring them to a counsellor who is known to have experience and expertise in that area, making you the obvious choice among possible referrals.

What's The Difference Between A Niche And Specialising?

They may overlap. However, a niche is more about the type of clients you want to work with; a specialisation is about the type of work you do. Specialising generally entails a specialist knowledge and skill which others in your field may not have. For example, you may choose to specialise in eating disorders, and choose a niche of adolescents. Or you might specialise in addiction, focusing on alcoholic men over 50. This Business of Therapy specialises in professional practice management and development, in the niche market of therapy practice.

Should I Generalise Or Specialise?

As time goes on, you may find yourself drifting towards a particular area of practice, a particular type of issue, a particular age group, etc. Some people are drawn from the outset to working in particular areas, for others it happens organically.

For example, I made a specific choice to start working with couples and sought out some training in that area. However, I found that I also attracted some clients in their early twenties and a high proportion of male clients. As time went on, much of my work began to focus on relationship issues. More recently, the mix is changing again, as I choose to work with professionals struggling to get their businesses off the ground.

If you find it difficult to identify a niche or special area of interest, refer to the list of possible niche and specialist areas on my website (http://thisbusinessoftherapy.com/possible-niches-or-areas-of-specialisation-for-therapists-2/ or http://tinyurl.com/jjjlse3) Choose a couple of areas from the list that you feel you have some ground in. Perhaps these might be areas that have personally touched you in your life, or were of relevance for clients you have worked with.

Some people are concerned about deciding on a speciality, believing it will limit the work available to them. However, this has not been my experience. Specialising allows you to focus your promotional materials; it does not mean that you will not attract any work outside of that area.

While it can be both professionally satisfying and financially rewarding to focus your efforts in one area of practice, I can remember a tutor advising us during training to keep a balanced portfolio. It can be difficult to control this, but it really is worth bearing in mind. I have said more about this in Balanced Portfolio Of Clients below.

One word of warning: Don't be misleading! From an ethical perspective, it may be inappropriate to present yourself as having expertise in a particular area unless you have established competence in it, either by specific training or studying in that area, or by experience. You might phrase it instead as a preference or interest of yours, or as a growing specialisation.

The Clients we Need

Many therapists believe that the clients that come to them bring, in addition to their presenting issues, some aspect of themselves that will help the therapist to learn and grow.

For example, I was taught growing up that it was rude to interrupt someone when they were speaking. I struggled therefore when some clients spoke continuously without a break, barely pausing to take a breath. Various supervisors patiently explained to me what I already suspected, that to talk continuously was a defence and that it was important for me not to collude with it. I was advised to draw the client's attention to the manner of their speaking. I experienced huge anxiety even at the thought of interrupting them, but gradually over time have become more comfortable with it. It rarely happens now that I encounter non-stop talkers in the work, but until I overcame my hesitation to interrupt, I continued to attract clients who would help me in that respect.

It does not follow that if you have a particular issue in your own life, you will necessarily find that issue in your clients. I find it is often more subtle than that. Invariably, though, I do find that I learn from each and every client.

Clients You Like To Work With

For a long time after I started my practice, I was afraid I wouldn't get further work if I turned anyone down. I was resistant to the idea that there are enough clients out there for me to be able to pick and choose. I was resistant to the idea that it was okay for me to say "I prefer this to this," as if saying so was somehow rejecting of people in need. If I was struggling with the work, I criticised myself for getting it wrong, or not working hard enough or told myself some other story. This meant that I ended up working with clients to whom perhaps I was not particularly well suited.

Following a spate of clients starting and then finishing prematurely, I started to reflect on what was going on for me. I found that I was working very hard in the sessions with some clients, trying to compensate for a feeling of inadequacy, a sense that I had nothing to offer. This sense grew if the client showed no change over a period of time. Some resentment coming from a sense of duty and obligation had begun to arise for me, as I struggled to balance my need to feel that I was being effective in the work with the recognition that my influence to change someone else is minimal.

Some time ago, I heard John Lonergan (former governor of Mountjoy Prison in Dublin) expressing it well. He said we can plant a seed in the ground and it may grow or it may not. We have no control over what grows. The seed will grow into the plant it is meant to be. We plant the seed, but there our influence ends.

I needed to let go of my need for the client to change, and to find a way of valuing my work, not only for what I give my client (although that too is important) but for myself. I can value what I do, even if the client does not. I can appreciate the subtle changes that may go unnoticed or unappreciated by the client. I can say I planted the seed, even if it fell on infertile soil, or has remained dormant to date.

Over time, as I began to clarify the sort of work I wanted to attract, the work coming to me began to change. I rarely have to turn people away, and I find that since becoming clearer about what I like and dislike, my practice is largely made up of clients that suit me, and who I suit. I believe that as I have become clearer about my identity in the work, and about my preferences, this has been communicated directly and indirectly to potential clients through my marketing efforts. I cover this topic more below.

Who Is An Ideal Client For Me?

A person with a problem has many choices about where they seek help. There are many people with problems who could benefit from your services. Not all of them will be an ideal client for you. Some of them may have issues that are outside your competence or skills. Some of them may impact you in a negative way. Some may be dealing with issues that are just too close to your own. Some may not be able to pay you.

So when you set out to promote your practice, you need to be *specific* about the clients and issues you want to work with. When you're clear about the clients you want, that message will come through in everything you do, whether you spell it out or not. Your website, your promotional materials, how you speak about your practice, will all give a consistent message.

Which means it's easier for potential clients to know if you're a good fit for them.

What I Learnt From Eddie Macken About My Ideal Client

I had never met Eddie Macken[9] in person but when I first saw him I knew at once that he was a master in the saddle. I was mesmerised by the way he held his hands, the way he sat, and by how effortless his movements appeared. Suddenly, all the directions my riding instructor had been giving me started to make sense. This is how it should look!

His horse was a beautiful beast, full of majesty and spirit. They cantered casually up to the six foot wall and jumped it as easily as if it was a pole six inches from the ground.

It was obvious when I thought about it. An experienced show jumper of Eddie's stature needs a mount to suit him. Eddie would have been bored by the gentle mare I ride. She suits me perfectly, but I couldn't hold his stallion for a moment.

However, it's not so obvious in the context of clients for a therapy practice. It is often said that "We get the clients we deserve," or "We get the clients we need." The implication seems to be that we have to work with any client because they are some part of a lesson we have to learn.

Perhaps. But what if the lesson is not that I have to find a way of working with this client no matter what, but instead that sometimes a client is just not a good fit for me?

Lots of people need help. But I may not be the best person to provide it.

One of the big advantages of being self-employed is that you get to choose what works best for you. And one of the big advantages of choosing the work more carefully is the possibility of enjoying the work so much more. By allowing ourselves the space to choose who we work with, and to pass on those that don't suit us to someone who is more suitable for them, we have a greater sense of ownership over our practice, leaving us free to be fully present in the work.

And what of the client? The client is also served as they get to work with someone who wants to be there with them, and can serve their needs, rather than someone who feels they have to be there.

Are The Therapist And Client A Good Fit?

While seeing a new client for the first time, I got a sudden sharp pain in my stomach. After the session, the pain continued on and off, and it was a couple of days before it was completely gone. I knew it was caused by stress. I could feel the tension throughout my body, and a sense of disconnection.

During the second session, I felt the same pain. I told the client that I was feeling discomfort in my stomach as he spoke, and sure enough, it was mirrored by something that he was also feeling.

The client rang to cancel shortly before our third session, and when I asked him why, he said he was not going to continue. I started to persuade him, and then stopped myself, and felt a sense of relief that I wouldn't have to feel that pain again.

It really was very strange, I thought, that having had such a strong physical reaction to working with this client, I was now trying to influence him to continue. I was also aware of the feeling of lack in me that was driving me to retain him as a client, as if there would never be another. As it happened, I was very busy at the time.

Reflecting afterwards, I realised that I didn't want to work with this client. I liked him, and could probably have been some help to him, but I didn't want to sit in the same room as him and feel that pain. I can't see being with someone that has such a painful effect on me can be good for either of us. At a minimum, it got in the way of me being fully present for him.

The truth was that I felt guilty about not wanting to work with him, and ashamed of both my reluctance and the guilt. So I covered it up by trying to hold onto him, even when he didn't want to stay.

There are benefits from working with a client who stretches us. However, this situation had taken me so far out of my range that I lost connection to myself. I was not the best person to help this client. At first I didn't realise that, but I'm glad that he did.

My wish for him is that he found someone who is better suited to him. My wish for myself is that in future, I'll be a bit more aware of listening to my body.

Putting Yourself Out There

For clients to find you, you must be willing to be found. It would be nice if clients magically turned up on our doorstep when we decided we were ready for them, but in my experience, most of us need to do more than just visualise a stream of clients. This means communicating with potential clients or referral sources that you are looking for clients.

How do you get the word out there? There are many, many routes to announcing that you are open for business. Here are some:

- Business cards
- Brochures
- Advertisements
- Entries in professional and local directories
- Sponsorship of local activities
- Articles in local newspapers or magazines
- Presentations or workshops
- Your own website, and
- Social media

These are all channels through which practices can communicate what they have to offer a potential client. If you don't know where to start, have a look at what other practices are doing, and see what draws you, and what you shy away from. I will talk about some of these options in more detail below.

Business Cards

When deciding on a design for your first business card there seem to be so many things to think about:

- How to describe yourself
- What colours and images to use
- How much information to include, etc.

It can be an issue that can keep people stuck for long periods of time while they work through their feelings about the options. In this way, it can reflect an underlying anxiety about getting started. Not having a business card can be a good reason for not taking the next step!

If you find yourself getting stuck on your business card, here are some thoughts for you to consider:

1. **Business Cards Can Serve in Several Ways:** They are a quick and easy way to share your contact details with potential clients or referrers. They can double as appointment cards. They can carry a message about your terms, for example, about cancellations. They can direct people to your website if you have one. Through the style and language, they also carry an indirect message about you and your practice.

2. **A Business Card Is A Tool, Not A Life-Long Commitment:** A business card is an essential tool for getting your name and contact details into circulation. And to achieve that goal, any business card is better than none. So if you find yourself agonising over it, my advice would be to start with something cheap and functional, which then buys you time to reflect at leisure on what you'd really like. Choose something plain and simple from Vista, Smile or one of the other low-cost printing websites, or ask your local printer for ideas, and use that in the short term. Once you have one business

card up and running, you can begin to explore different ideas for your next one.

3. **Your Business Card Makes a Statement About Who You Are:** Visibility can be uncomfortable. Invisibility may feel safer. However, it does not always serve. Your business card is an opportunity to say what differentiates you as a therapist from all the others out there. You can convey this directly through words or indirectly through the style or an image. In deciding on your business card, it can help to keep in mind the type of client you are trying to attract. Does your card reflect your ideal client? Or choose a couple of words that describe how you are in the work (for example, empathic, spiritual, clear, etc.) and ask yourself, does the card reflect that?

4. **What Information Should You Include?** There are no right or wrong answers to this question, but at a minimum, you will need to include your name, your phone number and address. Outside of that, do what feels right for you. Have a look at what other therapists have on theirs, and see what appeals to you, and what doesn't. Bearing in mind that space on the card is limited, consider (in no particular order):

   - Name
   - Practice name (if that's different)
   - Qualifications or accreditations

- Address

- Phone number

- Email address

- A photo of you

- An image or logo

- A map showing your location

- An inspirational quote

- The services you provide

- Date and time of next appointment

- A statement about cancellations/appointment changes

5. **Remember, It Probably Means More To You Than It Does To Your Client:** How much attention do you pay to other people's business cards? My guess is, unless you're getting ready to print your first business card, the answer is not much. If it's something you want to buy, you'll probably buy it, whether you like their card or not. If it's not, you may love their card, but it's unlikely to be a deciding factor. You can't know for sure the reactions of everyone who is going to see your business card, so my advice is, don't try. Focus on something that feels right for *you*, and fits with your values and beliefs.

6. **Choose A Business Card You Can Feel Proud Of:** If you find yourself reluctant to take your business card out in

public, you forget to bring cards to networking events, or if you feel embarrassed about it, then it's not working for you. Switch to something that you feel good about, and then that energy will translate itself to whoever you are talking to. Or practice handing your business card to a friend until you feel more at home with it.

7. **Get Help:** Explore the web for places where you can have logos and cards designed for you. Most of the online printing services provide templates you can use, as do local print or stationery shops. Fiverr.com is a website where you can buy a wide range of services for prices starting from US$5, including getting a logo or business card designed especially for you.

8. **Be Generous With Your Business Cards:** Don't skimp when deciding how many to get printed. The cost of printing each card reduces as you increase the quantity. It's a small cost with big potential.

9. **The Last Word:** Don't forget a card has two sides! Leave the back of your business card blank to have somewhere to write on. Or use the back for a favourite quote that says something about who you are in your work. Or show a map of your location, or a photo. Or better still, a statement about your business. For example, "It's never too late to get help," or "Every relationship can use a little support now and then."

What Do I Do With My Business Cards?

So your business cards are printed up, now what? Having put lots of energy into designing and printing your business cards, you may have no idea what to do next. Have you thought about ...

1. A business card can be printed onto a magnet. This could be given to doctors and other possible sources, for sticking to a filing cabinet. A paper card may get lost or thrown in the bin, a magnet is likely to remain in sight for longer.

2. If you've forgotten to bring your card with you, write your details on something that's to hand. This is better than saying you'll send your details on later because by the time your contact receives it, they may have forgotten who you are. You can always follow it up later as well, preferably in person.

3. Get used to having your cards close to hand, wherever you go. When you meet someone new, hand them out proudly and confidently. You never know when a contact may need your services, or want to give your details to someone else. If you're not proud of your card, ask yourself why. Maybe it's time to get a new one. If you can, shake the person's hand, and make eye contact as you give them your card. Smile!

4. A social occasion may not be the best time or place to have a business discussion. Acknowledge that, and give

your card, saying something like, "It's a bit awkward to talk now, but I'd love to meet up with you about this at a better time." Ask them when it would suit to call them, and ask for their card too.

5. When handing out your card, give three or four. If your contact likes you, they may pass your name on to someone else. If you feel comfortable enough to ask them to pass them on, do so. Keep your eyes open for places where you can leave a bundle of cards so people can pick them up. Someone may feel too shy or uncomfortable to ask, or they may not know that you're looking for more referrals. Hand your cards to local colleagues, who may be delighted to have the name of another therapist in the area to refer on to. Leave some with local small businesses who may be in a position to pass on your name, such as doctors, dentists, chiropractors, or physiotherapists.

6. Display your business cards in the room you work in, and in the waiting area if there is one. If you work in a centre, place a holder full of cards in all the public areas. You never know who might pick one up and pass it on or give you a call.

7. Take your business cards to workshops and conferences. Give them to everyone you talk to.

8. When writing to prospective referrers such as doctors, include your cards with your letters, so they can easily

pass your details on.

9. Hold on to business cards you get from other professionals, even if you're not interested in buying their services. At some stage, you may want to refer a potential client to them. You can also use them for ideas of different styles or designs, which may help you when you're redesigning your own, if only as an example of what you don't want.

10. Swap cards with anyone who might be a client or referral, or even someone whose work is interesting to you.

11. If you feel awkward with the idea of handing out and receiving business cards, practice with a friend until you're comfortable. If you're at ease, it helps others feel at ease too.

12. When someone gives you their business card, don't just pocket it. Take a good look and ask a question or make a comment about the style or design, the service they're offering or their business name. Acknowledge others by acknowledging their card.

13. Give some business cards to a client at the end of the first and last session. Someone who has first-hand experience of your work, especially if it has been a good experience, is a great referral source.

14.

Relationships With Local Doctors And Other Professionals

Doctors and other health professionals are a good source of referral. They are meeting patients who are vulnerable, often at times of crises, when counselling or therapy may be one of a range of possible supports. If you're not familiar with the doctors in your local area, make a point of getting in contact and letting them know you're open to accepting referrals.

Start by compiling a list of all the doctors in your local area from the Golden Pages, local directories and from the Internet. You might like to write to them in the first instance advising that you are in practice in the area. Your letter can set out your qualifications and the issues you deal with. Follow up your letter about a week later with a phone call. You may get to speak to the doctor, or more likely their secretary. Refer to your letter and ask to make an appointment to see the doctor to talk about the service you provide.

Be prepared for a mixed response to your request. Doctors are inundated with representatives of medical and pharmaceutical companies asking for their time. Some doctors like to keep appointments with anyone other than patients to a particular time of the day. Some don't make appointments at all, and some will ask you to come along and sit in the waiting room until they are free. Be prepared to be flexible. After all, if you make a good impression, it may help you down the road.

Bear in mind when sending out letters that your phone call

needs to follow fairly soon afterwards, and ideally an appointment soon after that. If the delay between your letter or call and meeting the doctor is too long, you will have to remind them of what you said in your letter or your call. Don't send out letters at such a pace that the follow-up isn't manageable for you. If you find it hard to speak to strangers on the phone, make a note of what you want to say before you call. Try it out with a friend or colleague first, and then stand up to make the call. Standing will help you to feel more confident and grounded.

When first setting up, I approached local doctors with my colleague Jennifer. We both found it hard, so we did the calls together. We set ourselves a goal for the number of calls we were going to make. She'd do one. Then I'd do one. And when we'd done our quota, we'd have coffee as a reward. As I've said a couple of times, having the support of someone else alongside you makes these things so much easier.

Not all doctors will see your work the way you do. Some medical professionals are very open to the idea of counselling and psychotherapy as a complement to their own work. And some are not. Others may be interested but not convinced of the merits of emotional work. Some see counselling or psychotherapy as too alternative, perhaps even a threat to what they do, and if this is the case, they may be a bit defensive. So while you want to get your point across, remember to keep it light. *Hard sell sells nothing.* You won't win everyone over to your way of thinking the first time you meet.

If you have been given an appointment, the doctor is probably somewhat open to the idea. A good rule of thumb is to focus on meeting the doctor where they are. Rather than trying to convince them of your perspective, use language that they can relate to, and avoid "therapy speak". Think about the situations they are facing in their practices, and where your work will support them. The medical model is one that is focused on diagnosis and prescription. If you can, describe your work in terms of the problems the doctor may be encountering, and the possible outcomes that can be expected.

Ask questions that draw out their views and how your work might support them in their work. Invite questions and comments on their experience of how patients may benefit from counselling and therapy. Don't try to convince them that you're right or that your way is the only one. Try instead to hold the place that there are many roads to healing, including both the medical and therapeutic ones.

If you feel that they have no interest in your service, don't waste your time. Finish up the conversation and leave. If there's a sense that they are interested, but a bit sceptical, go gently.

A good book full of practical advice about talking to strangers that is easy to read and absorb is *How to Win Friends and Influence People*, by Dale Carnegie. Although it is many years old, it is still worth reading.

Some doctors have no interest in meeting counsellors or

therapists but may ask you to send in some details. Have something ready in advance so that you can follow up your phone call. It doesn't necessarily have to be a glossy brochure. A one-page outline of your background, qualifications and experience, and the sort of issues you deal with will suffice. This will give you time to develop something more elaborate later if you wish, without delaying the process of making initial contact.

Preparing For Meetings With Doctors

So the doctor has agreed to see you. How can you prepare for the meeting? How do you convey to them what your work entails? What questions might they ask of you?

Here are some questions to help you prepare for conversations you might have with doctors or others who might refer clients to you. Think about them in advance of any meeting so that you have an idea of what you might like to say in response.

- What exactly do you do?
- What are your qualifications?
- How will that help my clients?
- Isn't counselling long and very costly?
- What outcomes can a patient expect?
- Do you work with medical card holders?
- What would you say to clients about medication for

depression?

- How would you work with a person who was suicidal?

- Do you do Cognitive Behavioural Therapy?

- What is the difference between your approach and…

- I already have a relationship with other therapists in this area. What are you bringing that is different?

If you find yourself with a doctor who expects you to make a presentation, you can speak from the answers you have prepared to these questions. If it's possible to do so within the limits of client confidentiality, try to give some examples from your work which show your skills and abilities. Again, the time to think about this is before your meeting.

Remember the medical model holds doctors as experts in the medical field, and they will be seeing you through this lens. In many ways, the idea of being an expert is contrary to the spirit of our profession, but you need to leave doctors with the assurance that their patients are in safe hands. Good preparation will help you build confidence.

Although it's not necessary, if you work with a particular speciality or issue it will help you to be more memorable than general practice. Again, doctors are familiar with the idea of a network of specialists. If you have a niche, you can prepare some of your presentation to focus on that area.

If you don't, focus your answers or examples around one or two areas that are most likely to be in the doctor's practice, such as depression, anxiety, or panic attacks.

When The Appointment Comes Around

When you're ready to meet with your local GP, what now? When you're there, in their office, what do you say? If this type of meeting is new to you, preparation is important to avoid feeling tongue tied. Here are a few thoughts to help you:

Before You Go, Prepare The Ground:

1. Have a clear idea of what you want to achieve from the meeting. What would you like them to learn from you? What do you want from them? What would tell you that the meeting has been successful for you both?

2. Have something prepared in advance, such as a few questions you can ask them, so that if the conversation is slow, you can use your questions to warm things up.

3. Keep it simple. Rather than flooding them with information, give a couple of generalised, anonymous examples of how your work has helped your clients.

4. Have some theory or research to hand if you find it supports you. Medicine is a science, and much of the progress depends on research.

5. If you do refer to research, consider handing a summary to the doctor rather than quoting from it. And

if they're interested in reading about it, offer to leave the details with them or to email them after the meeting.

6. In these situations, it always helps to have something tangible to leave with them. Bring brochures, business cards or flyers if you have them. If you don't have any, write up a one-page summary of the main points you want to get across, for example, ways in which counselling can help clients struggling with post-natal depression.

7. Consider doing GP visits with a colleague. It'll help you feel more confident and you can support each other.

When You Get There:

1. Remember you and the doctor are equals, in that you are both professionals; you are both skilled and experienced in your own field.

2. Try to hold an attitude of openness about whether you have something to offer each other.

3. Focusing on your breathing will help to ground you.

4. Be prepared for a wait. Even if you have an appointment, doctors will probably give priority to their patients. Bring something to pass the time.

5. Thank them for agreeing to see you (even if you have been waiting!) Shake their hand and smile (this will help you to relax.)

6. Take charge. You asked for the meeting, so continue the initiative by starting the conversation. Don't wait for them to do it for you. You might start with "I asked to see you because ...

   - I've recently set up locally and I wanted to let you know what services I provide; or

   - I work close by and I thought it would be helpful for both of us if we got to know each other; or

   - Although our work is very different, we usually have the same end in mind ... helping people to feel better."

7. If you work in a particular niche or speciality, say so. Doctors will be more likely to connect with you if you speak about a specific issue or client group (such as adolescents, elderly or women; with depression, post-natal depression, eating disorders, anxiety or panic), rather than a more general brief. Remember, there are other counsellors and therapists around, and this is one way to make you memorable.

8. Support the dialogue by asking about their perspective of counselling or psychotherapy:

   - Is this something that might be of benefit to your patients?

   - Have any of your patients availed of counselling before?

- How did it work out for them?

9. Anticipate their concerns, and bring them into the conversation:

    - What might prevent you from recommending counselling to your patients?

10. Be ready to address the most common concerns: It's too open ended, costly, lack of clear results, etc. Some useful arguments include:

    - Doctors are busy people and don't always have enough time to listen to patients in the way they need. Anyway, that's not really their work. Our work can complement the work of the doctor in this regard.

    - Change takes time. It may have taken years for a client to reach the current situation, and it will probably take time to turn it around.

    - Change won't happen without support, and significant change usually needs external support and structure, which counselling can provide.

    - People often get more value from things they pay for, than they do from what they get for free.

11. Make it easier for the doctors to recommend you, and their patients to contact you, by being flexible in what you offer. Consider:

- Offering a free consultation so the patient can find out if it's for them.

- Offering a fixed number of sessions as a block, perhaps at a slightly discounted rate. People often find it easier to commit when it's not so open ended.

- Leave business cards, brochures or flyers with the doctors. Putting them in a box or holder makes it easier for the doctor or their secretary.

12. Keep the focus on their needs and the needs of their patients rather than on your qualifications. You're a professional so the assumption will be that you are qualified.

13. You can ask a general question at the end, such as, "Is there anything else I can tell you about my work?"

14. Finish by thanking them again for making time to see you.

After you've left, send a short note or email, to thank them again, and send on any outstanding information.

Remember, while doctors can be an important source of work, they are not the only source. So don't rely solely on doctors for all your work. Some people may not consider their problem is one that requires medical treatment or may not want to receive medication and so may not bring it to the attention of their doctor.

Other Sources Of Work

Many clients will seek out a therapist or counsellor themselves, rather than coming through a doctor or other professional. How will these clients find you? This is where being willing to put yourself out there becomes important. There are two main channels for connecting with clients, online and offline.

My personal view is that the Internet is the place of first research for anyone under the age of fifty and probably a significant proportion of those over that age too. So it's a good idea to have a presence online.

Creating An Online Presence

Do you need to have a website? While this form of promotion is becoming more popular, many therapists do not have a website and seem to get by. So if this is a huge deal for you, don't scare yourself with it at the first instance; much can be done without one. If you feel overwhelmed by the idea of creating a website, keep it in mind for the future, when other promotional options have settled down a bit for you.

Without setting up a website, you can start to create an online presence by getting your name onto some of the many online directories on the Internet. See Internet Directories: Free and Paid Directories later in this section.

Another way of creating an online presence is to use other people's websites which allow you to post comments or discussion. For example, you could review a book on, say,

Amazon, relating to an area that you work with such as social anxiety, giving your name and a link back to your entry in an online directory. This is easier than it sounds!

Continuing to use social anxiety as an example, you could engage in a discussion by posting comments on a blog or website related to that issue. Perhaps you could take part in the discussion in the Yahoo Group dedicated to this topic. Don't post in a way that is purely promotional, focus instead on offering something practical such as resources that you have found to be useful. Other examples of where such online groups can be found are LinkedIn and Facebook. (See more at Social Media later in this section.)

Internet Directories: Free and Paid Directories

As I said above, another way of creating an internet presence without creating a website is by putting your name into the many online service and local directories that are out there. Often they are localised to an area, such as a directory of businesses offering goods and services in the Kildare area. They may also be grouped according to a service.

Many of these directories are free, and some have a charge for the listing. Among the paid sites, Holisto.com, WhatClinic and Natural Therapy For All are some of those popular among therapists. Before signing up to a paid site, it is useful to talk to other subscribers about their experiences. Some of the subscription directories guarantee a certain number of referrals per month as part of your subscription. Since the number of practices they promote is limited, and some of your subscription goes into giving those premium rate subscribers a higher profile, this might be good value for money.

To find online directories, try Googling "Counselling" and the location from which you intend to practice. Scroll through the search results that come up. Some of them will lead you to websites of other practitioners, and some will be other sources, such as directories.

I think of this sort of promotion as having a "drip, drip" effect. I think it helps to give your name or the name of your practice some substance if it comes up in more than one place on an internet search.

Professional Membership Directories

Don't forget to put your details up onto the website of any professional body of which you are a member. As I've said before, help out potential clients who would like to find you by being specific about any issues you work with and about any specialist training you might have.

One of the advantages of accreditation with a professional body such as IAHIP or IACP is that your name is included in their online directory of accredited members. This can prove to be a source of work and I have received several clients through both bodies of which I am a member. If you are a member of any other professional body (even one unrelated to therapy work), it might be useful for you to retain your membership and to keep some involvement, as work may come to you through colleagues (see Friends Or Colleagues later in this section.)

Getting Your Own Website

In order to get the most from an investment in a website, you do need to have a plan for promoting it, such as using Online Advertising or Social Media or investing in Search Engine Optimisation. Without some way of drawing people's attention, there's a danger that your website will be like one word in a Sunday newspaper, difficult to find and not very effective.

If and when you decide to get a website, there are different ways to get a website up and running. You can design and create it yourself if you have some computer skills, or you can employ a professional website designer and builder to do it for you. Which route you choose will depend on:

- The complexity of the site you wish to create

- Your own technical skills and confidence

- How much money you are willing to spend on the project, and

- How much time you have to spare.

Before leaping in, spend some time deciding what you want. Look at the sites of other therapists that you know and also some that you don't know. What appeals to you, and what doesn't? How do you respond emotionally to the images they use?

Get clear about the message you are trying to convey with your website. Is it directed mainly towards potential clients or more towards those who might refer clients to you? What will a visitor get from looking at your website? Are you educating them, or inviting them to work with you? What would you like them to feel as a result of looking at your website? Are you trying to convey peace or professionalism, or warmth? What colour schemes and styles do you like, and which would you pull away from? Make sure your contact details are clearly on show on every page. Ideally have some contact media, such as phone, email, etc.

If you have already got a logo, design or colour scheme for yourself (from your business cards perhaps), then you may wish to coordinate the two to create a brand image for your business. See also: Questions to Consider Before Choosing a Website below.

Creating Your Own Site

There are lots of websites that will help you to create your own website. Many of these will have you up and running for little cost. For example, WordPress allows you to create a basic site, with many styles and features to choose from. If you are willing to have a domain name (web address) that includes "WordPress" there is no direct charge. (Caveat: if you have a free site, and are lucky enough to have a lot of traffic through it, WordPress may post ads at the end of your pages, and in time you will be invited to go "ad-free" for a small fee.) If you don't want "WordPress" in the domain name, there is a small charge, at the time of writing about €15 p.a.

There are many other choices available. For example, Vistaprint offers a basic 3-page website that you design yourself, including hosting and domain name, for about €5 a month. They also have premium and professional options with 5 and unlimited pages respectively for about €10 or €15 a month. If you're short of funds and wary of doing it yourself, consider recruiting a transition year student to do it for you, or hire someone on Fiverr.com (basic charges from €5.50).

If you really are finding it hard to decide or commit, a good option might be to have a very simple website set up for you in the short term, to give you time to reflect on exactly what you want. Just include contact details and a brief overview of yourself and your practice.

No matter what you create it won't last forever so it will need to be updated and refreshed as time goes on.

Getting Your Website Created For You

When getting someone to do the work for you, it's probably even more important to have thought out what you want before you start. Read through Questions To Consider Before Choosing A Website below, before making your choice. To choose a provider, ask around. Speak to other therapists and ask them about their experiences. If you are choosing someone without a personal recommendation, ask them for examples of their work in similar businesses to yours.

One possible downside of getting it done professionally is that if there's a change in your phone number, work address or email address, you may have to go back to the supplier to get these done for you. Depending on the agreement you have, there may be a cost for this. Try to negotiate a deal that includes minor changes at no or minimal extra cost. Bear in mind that to attract traffic, there probably needs to be some dynamic (changing) content on the site and plan for this too.

Questions To Consider Before Choosing A Website

1. If you were looking for a therapist, what factors would influence your choice?

2. Who do you want to attract to your website? Who is your audience? (for example, GPs, other health professionals, other potential referrers, potential clients, etc.)

3. What result are you hoping to get? (More clients, client referrals, providing information, raising awareness, introduction)

4. If you are hoping to attract new clients by this, what are the characteristics of the clients you would like to reach? (consider: presenting issue, gender, age, attitude, ability to pay).

5. Does this website stand alone or will there be some other contact with the reader/receiver? Do you need to coordinate your contact to ensure consistency?

6. What questions might a reader have that you need to answer? For example:

   a) What do you do?

   b) How can you help me? What outcome can I expect to get from working with you?

   c) How long will it take?

   d) What is your approach (and what does that mean in layman's language!)?

   e) How often and how long are the sessions?

   f) Why should I hire you? What is unique or special about you?

   g) How much do you charge?

   h) How can I contact you?

   i) Other

7. What information do you want readers to have (but which they may not know they want/need)?

8. What words would capture the atmosphere or tone you'd like my marketing material to convey? (For example, professional, approachable, soulful, peaceful, etc.)

9. What might a satisfied client say about their experience of working with you?

Social Media

Whether or not you use social media to promote your practice will probably be determined by whether you use social media or not. Personally, I think if I were not in the business myself, I would be slow to acknowledge openly in social media my association with a counselling and psychotherapy practice. My fears of what others would read into it come to the fore. That is not to say that I would *not* "like" such a page, I just don't think I'd be as quick to acknowledge it as I would perhaps a less personal one.

I have to add, though, that the first time putting myself out there on Facebook, Twitter and LinkedIn was the hardest! At times, I can have an exaggerated sense of my own importance in the world, and imagine everyone is interested in and watching what I am doing. It's a humbling experience in many ways to spend hours agonising over the wording of a post, only to find that no one has read it.

Despite my obvious ambivalence, I have a presence on social media for both professional and personal use. I keep a professional presence on Facebook to remind my family, friends and former and present colleagues of what I do and where I can be reached. I hope that their sensitivity to being associated with the work I do will reduce with exposure as mine has. If someone says to a friend of mine, "I'm thinking of talking to a therapist about this," my hope is that my name will come to mind. Recently it happened that a former school friend who is a friend on Facebook, but with whom I have had no contact in at least twenty years, rang me to ask if she could pass my name to someone she knew. From reading what I had posted on Facebook, I seemed to her to be perfect for the job!

However, if you are cautious or resistant to engaging with these media by posting regularly and by revealing something of yourself, my view is, don't bother. The point of using these media for promotion is having a presence and being active. If you're uncomfortable with being active, you could find more productive uses for your time.

I have found LinkedIn to be a more useful site for me. There are many interest groups on LinkedIn, where you can connect with other professionals and members of your own and other bodies, and where you can post questions or queries. Some of the discussions can be interesting, covering clinical issues, and also practice management and development issues.

Advertising

Another way of promoting your practice is by advertising, through print media, television, radio or online. Print media include newspapers and magazines. Online advertising happens through Google and Facebook, or through paid advertisements such as the Golden Pages.

Advertising professionals will tell you that the return on your investment in advertising can be measured accurately by the number of calls that are received directly from the advertisement. However, the response to any promotion is influenced by many factors, such as

- The style and content of the writing
- The timing and placing of the advertisement
- The design and colour of the advertisement, the visual or aural impact.

If you intend to invest money in advertising, it may pay to invest first of all in professional advice about some of these issues.

Gary Craig, Founder of EFT, tells a great story to illustrate the fickle power of advertising. A friend of his had a small holiday home in the mountains which he rented to the public. For some time, it was advertised as a *small cottage* and he was disappointed by the poor response. When he changed just one word in the advertisement, describing it as a *cabin* rather than a cottage, the number of enquiries multiplied and he never looked back!

Print Advertising

One obvious form of advertising to consider is print advertising. The questions you might ask yourself are:

- What publications should I be aiming for?
- What is the readership (in numbers, age group, locality, etc.)?
- What sort of return on my investment would tell me it's

been a success?

Again, consider what feels right for you. Don't choose a publication that you don't feel attracted by, even if it has worked for someone else. If you don't like the publication, then you are unlikely to resonate with its readers. Small local papers and magazines are likely to be less costly and more focused than the nationals. Consider too, specialist publications that will be read by your ideal clients, such as those directed towards new mothers or older readers.

When we first set up, my colleague Jennifer and I tried advertising for about a year in a local paper, and while we received a small number of queries, neither of us felt the return justified the cost. However, other colleagues have found the same publication to be a successful route for them, proving that experience differs.

If you can write and have the interest to do so, a less costly way of getting exposure in a print medium is to offer an article on some subject that might be of interest to readers and at the same time draw attention to the type of work that you do. This is unlikely to appeal to the national papers, but smaller local or community magazines may be grateful for some input. You might, for example, offer an article about the stress that can be experienced in families around particular times of the year, and a few tips on how to deal with it.

The professional bodies are also open to receiving articles of interest, particularly if you operate in a specialised niche.

These publications will tend to raise your profile with referrers rather than potential clients.

Online Advertising

An increasingly popular advertising medium is internet advertising, and by this I mean Google Ads or similar. This form of advertising works by popping up an advert for your practice when someone does a search for a keyword or phrase that you have chosen. The keyword may relate to the locality or a niche area of practice. Generally, you pay according to the number of times your advertisement is clicked on by interested browsers. This is not a guarantee that when someone clicks onto your website that they will follow through with an enquiry or become a client, but it does increase the traffic to your website.

Internet advertising requires some level of engagement from you if you are to get the best results for your money. The more generic the keywords and phrases you use, the more expensive the ad will be. To get the best value for your money, you need to be willing to play around with the wording of the ad to see what works best. So, if technology is not your thing, this may not be the route for you. You may be able to get some help with it from companies that specialise in Search Engine Optimisation. One practitioner who extensively uses internet advertising has written for my blog, and you can read about his experience on my blog at http://thisbusinessoftherapy.com/advertising-your-therapy-practice-on-the-internet/ or http://tinyurl.com/zjr9vzy

Golden Pages

Another form of advertising to consider is the Golden Pages. Golden Pages is published in both print and online versions. The online version features quite highly on the ranking when an internet search is conducted. As the directory is arranged geographically, you will be competing with other services in the same area. If you are in a large area, consider paying for the premium service which shows your business higher in the rankings, and being more specific in the details you give, to differentiate you from others.

Radio And TV

Some practitioners have used local radio and TV successfully to promote their practices. These are typically practitioners who have developed an expertise in a particular area and have become known for their willingness to comment publicly on issues related to that topic.

Former and Existing Clients

Referrals do come through former and existing clients, and as long as boundaries are appropriately observed, this can be the best types of recommendation. A client will recommend you if they are finding the work is helpful to them, so someone coming to you through this route has already received a positive impression, which can help in the creating of the relationship.

An accountant I know uses the slogan "Clients Recommend Us" in all his promotional literature. Curiously, I find that I recommend him too, proving the power of positive suggestion. I suspect that more people talk about their accountants than their therapists (there still remains some stigma attached to undergoing therapy), but the idea is a useful one, giving a strong message about the quality of service provided, and the level of satisfaction received.

Friends Or Colleagues

Again, it is important to ensure that in taking referrals from friends or colleagues, boundaries are appropriately preserved. However, that safeguard aside, friends and colleagues can be an important source of work. We are not always going to be able to take every client that comes our way. Ethical restrictions will deter most therapists from taking on as clients our own friends, neighbours and family members, or close connections of our existing clients. Complicated issues may require specialised knowledge or training. Therefore, we all need to have a network of people to whom we can refer. And network connections work both ways!

A good start to establishing such a network begins with those you trained with, fellow students and tutors. It can be added to with colleagues you meet at courses or conferences.

It is also a good idea to think of people you may have worked with or had contact with in previous roles, and who may have the opportunity to refer clients to you. Perhaps a friend or neighbour of theirs is looking for a therapist?

Make a list of everyone you know who fits into the above categories, and start making contact with a couple of them every week. Have a brief chat on the phone, or arrange to meet up for coffee or lunch if you prefer. Try to spend at least a little of your time together talking about your practices.

Many smaller organisations do not have a formal employee assistance programme, but may from time to time need the help of a professional for one of their staff who may be struggling. It is in a company's interest to support a staff member who is experiencing difficulties, as this can speed their return to work, and to a more productive attitude. Issues such as bullying or harassment within the workplace, or family issues, may impact on the workplace. Perhaps a friend or neighbour works for such an organisation and could suggest your name?

Other Networking And Promotional Activities

Attendance at courses, conferences and professional body meetings or events can help to expand your contacts. "Meetup" groups (check them out on the Internet) are a central source of information where groups of like-minded people can come together. Try to think broadly about how you could spread the word. You could invite members of the public to an open evening at your place of work. You could offer introductory talks on popular subjects within your area of work, for example, coping with depression or managing anger.

Business Network International is a formal networking organisation specifically focused towards generating referrals and contacts for small businesses. It involves a local group of business people and professionals, in which members agree to refer enquiries to other members of the group. There is a charge for membership. I know professionals (therapists and others) for whom this has been an important source of work, especially in the start-up phase.

Other examples of promotional and networking activities include anything where you get to interact with professionals who may be able and willing to pass work to you, or with people who may get to know you and refer themselves to you. Examples of such activities include involvement in local social or community projects, for example, sports clubs, St Vincent de Paul, youth projects or the Lions Club. You could offer your services to local secondary schools to contribute to their careers guidance programmes, through speaking to students or conducting mock interviews. You could participate in support groups for families who have experienced struggles of any sort. Keep an open mind, and pay attention to what interests you.

Is It Possible To Promote My Practice In An Ethical Way?

Many therapists find it hard to promote themselves and their practices. We have all had experience of sleazy, pushy marketing or sales in the past, so it is understandable to fear visiting that experience on others. People looking for therapy or counselling may be feeling vulnerable already; no one wants to take advantage. We have little control over how the client may experience therapy or of the outcomes clients may expect. Therapists are also wary of breaching the ethical guidelines set down by the professional bodies and may err on the side of caution.

So there's a dilemma. If you want to share your work with the world and help more people, you have to let those people know you're willing and available, but can you do that in a way that is ethical, authentic and in line with your values and principles?

When you're considering what to say or write, think about the following ...

1. **Avoid guarantees about the outcome of the work.** Dramatic claims about results, such as mending broken hearts, curing depression or overnight eternal happiness are all likely to be exaggerated! On the other hand, you probably offer kind, attentive listening, an opportunity to explore old patterns and beliefs that no longer serve, and a chance to get something off their chest.

2. **How will your colleagues and friends see your actions?** Also known as the *Irish Times* test. If you'd be happy for someone to write about it on the front of the daily newspapers, it's probably okay to do or say it! Take care, however, that you don't use this measure as a reason not

to take action.

3. **What would your professional body say?** Would you be comfortable defending your action or what you've said if you were challenged by your professional body?

4. **Don't claim to be more than you are.** Do you use designatory letters to imply that you have qualifications which aren't rightly yours? Do you imply you are accredited when you're not? Are you entitled to describe yourself as you do? Be honest about your qualifications and experience.

5. **How do others promote themselves?** Consider others in the same field, and also organisations (for example non-profit or charitable ones) that you admire, and whose ethics are in line with yours. How do they describe themselves? Can you see them talking about their work as you talk about yours?

6. **Are you promoting yourself by denigrating others?** Don't criticise your competitors. The golden rule applies here: "Do as you'd like to be done by."

7. **Is it ethical not to market your services?** This interesting question is worth sitting with. If there are people out there who you could help, is it okay not to offer your help?

One Last Thought About Growing Your Practice

Earlier in this book, I wrote about the sort of products you are selling and asked you to think a little about that. Most of this chapter has been about how to attract therapy clients.

However, income can also be earned in other ways which, though not strictly therapy work, are broadly related to your work as a therapist. Think of your therapy work as the core or root of your practice, and other services could be connected to or growing from, or indeed feeding that core. Related services might be provided to employers, health care providers, policy makers, therapy schools and so on.

For example, you might teach a class that is in part related to your work, which might support your practice by:

- Additional income from the teaching

- Raising your profile as having some knowledge or expertise in the area

- Bringing clients who have attended the class, or people they know.

In another example, you might write articles for a professional journal in an area in which you have some knowledge, again raising your profile among your peers, who may be in a position to refer work. You may receive payment for this or you may not, depending on the publication's policies.

Conclusion

In short, there are many ways in which the work can come to you, and many ways in which you can announce your presence so that clients may find you. Keep an open mind, and try not to close off avenues that might yield results. Watch what others are doing and see if something similar would feel right for you.

Be open to your own ideas, or to ways in which the not so obvious approaches can be adapted. Allow your own sense of creativity to generate interesting and novel ways to promote your practice.

In addition to the obvious channels, I think it's useful to keep your focus on where you can be of service to others. Give generously to others where you can, because while those you give to may not return the favour directly, the energy you invest will come back to you through some other route. A hand held open is able to both give and receive. A closed hand can do neither.

Exercise: Marketing Plan

Review this chapter again, and as you do make notes about the principle elements of how you are going to market your practice using the following questions to prompt you.

What services do you plan to provide for your clients? (e.g. counselling, psychotherapy, etc.)

To what people are you going to provide your services? (e.g. individuals, couples, groups; adults, adolescents, children)

In what format do you plan to provide these services? (e.g. contract: open-ended, fixed, short term, long term; media: face to face, phone, Skype, email)

What are the main issues you'd like to work with? (e.g., relationships, addiction, anxiety, etc.)

Who is your ideal client?

How would you like prospective clients to see you? (e.g. as expert in the field of their concern, or as expert in a particular therapeutic approach, or as a warm professional who can relate to their pain, etc.)

What would tell you that your marketing activities have been effective? (e.g. X no. of clients in a year from now)

Through what route do you see your clients finding you? (e.g. referral from doctors or other professionals, through advertising or promotion by you, meeting you at some event or function)

List three channels through which you can make yourself known to your target market:

1

2

3

List three small steps you can take in the next week to promote your practice:

1

2

3

Part 7:

The Fourth Pillar: Managing Your Practice

MANAGING

Anticipate the difficult by managing the easy.[10]

> **Goals:** Order and harmony, smooth running
>
> **Key tasks:** Create processes and structure
>
> **Key mindset:** Discipline

The fourth pillar is where the routine housekeeping tasks get done, such as the bookkeeping and the cleaning. These tasks are not generally either big or difficult, but the absence of their being done can create problems.

Any business has many such small tasks that require attention, thinking about and maintenance. In a typical therapy or counselling practice, bills need to be paid, insurance needs to be renewed, supplies need to be bought for the bathroom and the kitchen, the diary or bookings need to be managed, the books need to be written up and tax returns prepared.

The essence of this pillar is accepting that these chores are part of the work of being self-employed. You will need to set some time aside in your working week to ensure they get done. In the early stages, the time investment will be greater as you learn the processes and structures that suit you, and you familiarise yourself with what needs to be done.

Most schools of therapy focus on teaching trainees how to work with clients. The skills necessary to create a business around the core education are not generally taught. This phenomenon is also present in most other professions. Consequently, many therapists who choose to be self-employed find themselves stuck in a place where they are really good at the client work, but with little or no idea how to create a business model that works for them.

If you are going to flourish in your therapy practice, as I hope you will, then I would encourage you to include in your continuing professional development some training and education about business management. Congratulations. Reading this book is a great first step in growing your awareness of the information and skills you may need; however, it is only a beginning. As your practice develops, you will encounter specific challenges which may require you to learn more than this introduction can give. There are many other low-cost and free options around. Try the books and digital resources in your local library or the many online courses available on UDEMY.com or similar websites. You will find some suggested reading material on my website at http://thisbusinessoftherapy.com/like-to-learn-more-about-the-business-of-therapy-heres-a-reading-list/ or http://tinyurl.com/je53we4

The Three Stages of a Therapy Practice

All businesses grow through a series of distinct phases. Whether it's a global manufacturer, a local bakery, or a professional practice, every business starts somewhere and develops into something else. Living things also go through these stages. A seed grows into a sapling, then later to a mature tree. A person starts as a group of cells, grows into a baby, a child and adolescent, and finally emerges into an adult.

These three stages are linked by periods of growth and development. To move from one stage to the next certain developmental hurdles need to be overcome. Some challenges need to be met. Some lessons need to be completed. And while these processes are taking place, the plant, the young human or the professional practice has needs that must be met to ensure that the growth progresses.

A child needs a committed parent, who is attuned to their needs, and is desirous of the child's achieving their own potential to thrive. Without a parent to provide appropriate shelter and nourishment, love, encouragement and holding, the child cannot thrive. In the absence of these essential needs being met the growth and development of a child will be impaired, and their ability to function in the world as an adult may be restricted.

In the same way, if a budding therapy practice is not carefully tended and nurtured the practice may never fully thrive, or reach its full potential.

In talking about a professional practice, the stages of development can be identified as follows:

At the baby or seedling stage,

- There is an outline concept or vision of the practice to come, but this needs to be developed and its potential realised.

- The identity of the practice is still vague and uncertain, core values are still being developed, boundaries are being consciously applied.

- The practice is fragile and vulnerable and needs a lot of attention and support to survive.

- The practitioner is heavily dependent on the support of a supervisor or others with more experience.

- Unexpected or significant challenges may wipe out the practice.

- The flow of work is uncertain, sources of work are unpredictable, strategies and processes for generating work are erratically applied.

- The finances of a seedling practice could be described as "less than enough," in that income is irregular and insufficient to meet basic costs.

- The practitioner is excited about doing the work and helping clients in need, impatient to get going, but frustrated at the slow progress. They may be easily disheartened when things go wrong.

At the adolescent or sapling stage,

- The vision or concept has begun to be realised, its potential beginning to take shape. Core values are beginning to emerge.

- The identity of the practice has begun to emerge, perhaps evidenced by a growing reputation.

- Workflow is more constant but still irregular, sources of work are beginning to emerge, processes and strategies are beginning to settle into practices.

- The practice is less fragile and vulnerable, but still needs considerable support.

- The influence of supervisors and significant others is beginning to give way to the practitioner's emerging trust in their own judgement.

- The financial situation of the practice can be described as "just about enough," in that income meets basic costs, but there is little or no surplus.

- The practitioner is more confident of his/her abilities to generate work and more trusting in the continuing presence of sufficient work, but unexpected setbacks still have a big negative impact.

On average, over a period of 3-5 years, a healthy, well-supported practice will survive the early stages, and grow into a mature practice.

- The therapist has a clear understanding of the identity of their own practice, and the work that suits them.

- They will also trust their own judgement in the work, but also in the significant decisions about their own practice.

- Financially speaking, a healthy and mature practice can easily and consistently meet its day-to-day expenditure.

- The practitioner will be able to invest in activities that support continued growth (such as a planned marketing campaign).

- Work will flow in to the practice constantly and predictably, and sources of work will be well established.

- The practice will create sufficient surplus income to enable provision to be made for the future, for example, through retirement.

- The mature practice will also have the resilience to take the ups and downs of the economy in its stride.

- The practitioner will feel confident of his or her abilities not just to help clients, but also to run and manage their own business including their ability to generate work.

Your goal when starting out in practice is to move over time to the mature or "more than enough" stage. Some practitioners will achieve the more than enough stage quicker than others, but there really is no prescribed timetable, as we each grow at a different rate. You will, however, need to have some sort of a plan to achieve the more than enough stage, and be willing to take the necessary action because it is most unlikely to happen without your commitment and willingness to stretch.

It is your job to be the parent or guardian of this young practice, helping it through its early years.

The biggest factor influencing the progress of your practice through the stages of development is your internal environment, and particularly your feelings, values and beliefs around creating a sustainable business. Without a nurturing and supportive internal structure, you are unlikely to take the actions necessary to grow your practice.

Our financial situation may be an indicator of whether we have unresolved issues around money or self-worth. In particular, our attitudes to money and wealth, how it is acquired and used, and our beliefs about our worthiness and deserving, not just of money, but of love and support, contribute to the ground and the soil in which we grow our young practices.

Many things can get in the way of moving from one stage to the next, and they may not seem to be directly connected. How we interact with our clients, our friends and families, how we see our roles and responsibilities can all have a direct impact on our ability to generate income. So too, our religious beliefs, our attitudes toward authority, our physical health, and many more can be relevant factors.

Money rarely makes us happy, but it can go a long way to helping us to feel secure, and having enough money certainly gives us more options than having none. Equally, the lack of money, or living in debt or fear of debt, can add hugely to the stress levels we feel. Trying to grow a practice from a place within ourselves of financial need or pressure may actually inhibit our ability to achieve the growth we desire.

To move from stage to stage, you need to put in place:

- An idea of where you want to get to.

- A plan to make it happen. Practices do not create themselves.

- A process to review what you are doing and how it is working, and to identify any changes you need to make.

- A network of support in the form of supportive or like-minded people who appreciate you and what you do.

If you find yourself stuck at the "just enough" or "less than enough" stages, it will greatly benefit you to explore your relationship with money. For more on this subject, you may like to read the following articles on my website:

- Common Beliefs about Money and Wealth: Part 1 (http://thisbusinessoftherapy.com/truth-or-myth-common-beliefs-about-money-and-wealth-part-1/) or http://tinyurl.com/jad5evv

- Common Beliefs about Money and Wealth: Part 2 (http://thisbusinessoftherapy.com/truth-or-myth-common-beliefs-about-money-and-wealth-part-2/ or http://tinyurl.com/h7lb8l6)

- Kibera (A short stretch of my personal journey to resolve conflicts and confusion around money) (http://thisbusinessoftherapy.com/kibera/ or http://tinyurl.com/gkqjr78)

I will speak more about these issues in Part 9: The Sixth Pillar – Valuing Your Practice

Housekeeping Issues

Whatever the shape of your practice, big or small, in your home or in a centre, certain tasks will have to be addressed. I think of these as housekeeping. They include, for example, keeping your client records, doing what is needed for the maintenance of your qualification, accreditation and re-accreditation, maintaining your financial books and records and submitting your tax return, and ensuring you have adequate PII.

Client Records

Check with your own professional body about the length of time for which you are required to keep your client notes. They should be stored in a secure place, where the client's privacy is assured, such as a locked cabinet or press.

The big debate about client records when I was training was around their potential for discovery and use in legal action taken by a dissatisfied client. Personally, I think it is too narrow a perspective, and a focus on the rather slim possibility of the dangers of writing and keeping client notes limits the potential benefits of this discipline. On the other hand, some therapists have been called to produce their notes in court, and you need to think about this when deciding what you should and should not include in your notes.

When I was involved in the accountancy profession, a similar debate took place. Some firms took an extreme view, retaining minimal records of the work performed. In time, they found that this was, as the saying goes, cutting off their nose to spite their face, and in time, a balance emerged.

In the event of some form of legal challenge, having no written records may protect you (and perhaps the client) from something that could be used against you. However, no one's memory is perfect, and your notes may also protect you. While legal challenge can be hugely disruptive and stressful when it happens, the incidence of therapists being sued is relatively small. The benefits of writing and maintaining client notes, for me at least, far outweigh the danger that they will be used against me. And, while the records might be used by someone in a case against me, they can also be used by me in my own defence, so it cuts both ways. It is very much a matter of what works for you.

In practice, I rarely refer back to client notes, preferring to adopt instead a strategy of meeting the client where they are on the day we meet. However, I stress that this is a personal choice, and I know many therapists who like to review their notes of previous sessions, as it keeps them focused. On the odd occasion that I do a review with clients, the notes can be a useful reminder of where the work has gone, what the client's original aspirations were, and the journey that has been taken. They can also be useful in the final stages of the work, in reflecting again on the journey the client has taken. For those clients who choose to do some of their work through art, and for whom I keep the resulting artwork, those pieces can themselves be a useful pictorial representation of what has happened.

Data Protection

You should also be aware of the requirements of the Data Protection legislation, details of which you can find at https://www.dataprotection.ie/docs/A-Guide-for-Data-Contollers/y/696.htm or http://tinyurl.com/z7y7xrv .

Practice Books And Records

Some therapists do not like to hear their therapy practice referred to as a business. However, the Revenue Commissioners certainly consider it to be a business and, therefore, will expect the appropriate financial books and records to be maintained. If you have never done any bookkeeping, I suggest you spend a little bit of time becoming familiar with this aspect of your practice. While you are still at the early stages, you will have fewer transactions and more time than you will have later in your professional career.

It is your responsibility to advise the Revenue that you are in business and to prepare and submit the appropriate tax returns. It is not up to the Revenue to ask or prompt you, and there are significant penalties for non-compliance, both financial and reputational, including the threat of having your details published in the national newspapers. It is possible that you may be the subject of Revenue Audit and your books and records may come under close scrutiny. While this may only be the experience of a small number of taxpayers, perhaps you should not rely on the odds!

If you are open to working with computers, a simple spreadsheet is more than adequate for a small professional practice. I use Microsoft Excel. The advantage of a computer program like Excel is that it takes a lot of the drudge out of the task because it does the calculations for you. The basics are easy to learn. Microsoft Works (a scaled-down, simplified version of Excel) is often available free of charge and pre-installed when you buy your computer. It is also available for smart phones and tablets so that you can keep up to date when you're on the move. There are also many bookkeeping packages that you can buy, or use online for a small fee, which are suitable for a small professional practice.

If you are not comfortable using a computer program, a simple handwritten list of your income and outgoings will form a good basis for your accounts.

At a minimum, your records should include:

- A record of the fees received: date, name or code and amount

- A record of the expenses paid out: date, name, nature of the expense, the amount, and how it was paid (cash, credit card, cheque, etc.)

- An annual income and expenditure account, summarising the transactions for the year.

I suggest you use a separate bank account for your business. It makes it much easier for you (or for an accountant, or the Revenue in the event of an audit) to see the transactions that need to be included in the end of year accounts. Lodge your receipts in full to your business account, and pay any costs directly from the account by cheque or account transfer. That way, your bank account forms the basis of your end of year accounts. If you pay expenses from the fees you receive in cash, or if your personal expenses are mixed up with your business ones, you will find it more difficult to pull the figures together at the end of the year. There is an additional cost to running another bank account, but this is small in comparison to the advantages.

Quite apart from the practical considerations, there is a psychological advantage to having a separate account for your practice, in that it reinforces the idea that your practice is a business, and helps you to look at it in this way.

Make a habit of writing up your records regularly. The Revenue will expect you to be able to establish the state of the business at any time, so the records do need to be reasonably current. It is also much easier to remember what a particular receipt or expense is a couple of weeks after it happens than it is a year later! Keep any receipts or invoices for the costs you incur, even small cash expenses. I have a pocket in the back of my diary into which I slip any small papers connected with my work, and when it gets full, I transfer them to a more permanent folder. Then later, when time allows, they are sorted and written up.

Expenses that you may incur in your practice include:

- Room rental and associated costs such as light and heat, rates, repairs, cleaning

- Supervision

- Additional training or CPD

- Technical books or journals

- Professional subscriptions paid to membership bodies such as IAHIP or IACP

- Motor expenses (note: not all motor expenses incurred in your business will be allowed for tax purposes)

- Stationery, such as business cards, headed notepaper, record books

- Advertising or promotion, including costs of a website or printing of flyers, etc.

- Professional indemnity or other insurance

Separately, you may need to keep records of client hours. These may be needed for a variety of reasons including accreditation or re-accreditation, if you work with therapy students, or for other reporting purposes.

While nobody wants to consider themselves at risk for a legal action, bear in mind that any records may be subject to scrutiny, should you be unfortunate enough to find yourself in that situation. You should keep your accounting records and related documentation (including bank statements) for at least six years after the accounting year end to which they relate.

Making it Easier for Yourself

If you feel overwhelmed by the prospect of doing your accounting, there are lots of things you can do to make it easier for yourself.

Let Your Diary Double As Your Income Record

For most therapists, their practice life is organised around appointments. Use your diary to record what you receive from clients and for what's owed but not yet paid. If you keep your diary on your phone or other device, perhaps you could use an app that allows you to download the details to your computer.

Let Someone Else Keep The Records For You

If you're not familiar with bookkeeping, it might be easier to get someone to do it for you. Find a local bookkeeper in the Golden Pages or online. Alternatively, perhaps you know a college or transition year student who would like to practice their bookkeeping skills. Your accountant may also provide this service for you, or direct you to someone who can do it.

Technology Is Your Friend

Whatever the task, technology has a solution for it! There are lots of apps available to help you with your bookkeeping. Use online banking wherever possible to pay bills and transfer money (all the major banks provide this facility). You can generally export the transactions from your online bank account into Excel, making it easier to write up your books. Try out online accounting software to simplify your bookkeeping (for example, Sage or the Big Red Book). There are also apps in which you can keep track of your cash expenditure. There are oodles of options, look around and find the ones that suit you best.

Tax Returns

This is not a book about taxes or finances, and I am not a practising tax advisor, so I am not going to enter into detail here. You may need to consult an accountant.

It is your responsibility to make a return. It is not the responsibility of the Revenue Commissioners to elicit or demand a tax return from you. Income Tax is based on the calendar year, and returns are due to be submitted by 31st October for the previous year to 31st December. Tax is payable to the Collector General in two instalments, preliminary tax by 30th June and the balance by 31st October. The deadline for submission is extended by two weeks if you file and pay any tax due through the Revenue's online system, ROS.

So, for the year ended 31st December 2016, your Preliminary Tax is due to be paid by 31st October 2016 and any balance due by 31st October 2017. Your tax return for that year should be submitted by 31st October 2017 (or 14th November 2017, if you use ROS.)

If you think you are likely to have a tax liability, you might consider setting up a standing order so as to spread the payment throughout the year.

What Expenses are Allowable for Tax Purposes, and What Are Not?

I am often asked this question by practitioners. I must reiterate here that I am not a practising accountant, nor a tax expert, so this should be used as guidance rather than Gospel! Ultimately, what is allowable is decided by the Revenue, taking into account your specific circumstances.

The guiding principle is "... *wholly, exclusively and necessarily for the purposes*" of your profession.

- **Post start-up costs:** Only those expenses that are incurred AFTER you start to practice are allowable.

- **Rent and Rates:** If you rent your premises, then these costs are allowable. If you use your home, you may be able to claim some portion of these costs, but see the caveat below.

- **Light and Heat:** Again, if you rent your premises and incur these costs, they are allowable. If you work from home, some portion of the costs of heating and lighting your home may be allowable, but again, see below.

- **Repairs and Maintenance (but not of a capital nature):** Capital costs are major purchases of premises, furniture and fittings. Those costs are not allowable. Repairs and upkeep (examples: plumbing repairs, roof repairs but not replacement, electrical repairs) are allowable.

- **Insurance:** Professional indemnity insurance and other insurances directly related to your work are allowable. Personal insurances such as life insurance, medical insurance or pension contributions may afford you some credit against your tax liability, but are not directly allowable.

- **Training costs (CPD) and reference books:** Workshops and seminars related to your work are allowable, as are the costs of travelling to them. So too are reference and text books.

- **Membership and journal subscriptions:** Professional subscriptions related to your work, such as IAHIP or IACP, are allowable. Unrelated subscriptions, including union membership, are not allowable. Subscriptions to professional journals related to your work are allowable.

- **Professional fees:** Professional fees incurred that are related to your work are allowable, e.g. supervisor, accountant or lawyer.

- **Bank interest and charges:** Bank charges related to a business account and interest paid on work-related loans are allowable.

- **Travel/motor:** Only the travel expenses incurred from your place of work to the client are allowable.

- **Consumables:** Costs such as stationery, candles, tissues, light bulbs are all allowable.

- **Promotion:** Costs incurred in promoting your business, such as advertising, website, business cards, or promotional activities are also allowable.

What Costs Are Not Allowable for Tax Purposes?

- **Pre-start-up costs:** Costs incurred before you set up in practice are not allowable, even if they relate to the business.

- **Travel to and from business premises:** Driving or travelling from your home to your place of business is not allowable for tax purposes.

- **Capital costs:** The cost of buying premises or a car, or a major replenishment of premises is not allowable.

- **Expenses not related to business:** Only those costs that relate to your business are allowable. For example, if you are working from home, all the costs of keeping and running your home are not allowable. Costs that allow you to go to work, such as child care, are not considered to be related to your business.

- **Personal therapy:** The cost of self-care, including the cost of personal therapy, is not generally allowable.

- **Union dues:** Unless it is a specified condition of your employment or associate status that you be a member of a union, such costs are not allowable.

Caveat: Claiming Expenses When You Work From Your Home

A word of warning about working from home and claiming expenses for tax purposes. You can claim a portion of the costs of running your home against your income for tax purposes if you are using part of your home as your workplace. So, for example, you could claim a portion of the costs of lighting, heating and insuring your home against the income you receive from your therapy practice.

This would normally be done by finding a reasonable way of proportioning those costs between work related and not work related. For example, you could take the floor area of the room you use for work, say 100 sq ft, and divide it by the total floor area of your home, say 1,000 sq ft. Then apply this proportion to the cost, i.e., one-tenth of the costs. This method assumes that the room is not used for other purposes when you are not seeing clients there. If it is used for other purposes, say on three days a week, the proportion is further reduced by that. So, using the figures above, if your total relevant expenses are €500 for the year, €50 could be claimed against your income if the room is not otherwise used, or if the room is being used on the other days, €21 could be claimed.

However, claiming expenses for your home could bring some unintended expenses, too. You might find that you could be assessed for business rates, or that the Principal Private Residence Exemption for Capital Gains Tax purposes could be threatened. If the amounts involved are significant, talk to a tax expert before making a claim.

How To Structure Your Therapy Practice

What structure do you imagine for your therapy practice: sole trader, partnership or company? Most therapy practices are sole practices, i.e., one person practising on their own. A much smaller number operate as partnerships (two or more people practising as a unit), and fewer still practice as limited liability companies.

The main difference between these choices is a legal one, and relates to what happens if the practice becomes insolvent (i.e., if you go broke!). In the case of a sole tradership, the practitioner will be personally liable for all the debts of the practice. So if a dissatisfied client sues, and is successful, the practitioner runs the risk of losing any personal assets such as their home (even if they did not practise from it), car, shares or bank accounts. A sole trade means you get to make all the decisions on your own terms, in your own time. You're not accountable to anyone but yourself!

On the other hand, you may lose out on the advantages of a group of people working together; the whole being greater than the sum of the parts. The big advantage of working in a partnership is the wider range of experience, expertise, skills and knowledge that a bigger structure can bring. For example, one therapist may specialise in working with couples, another with children, a third with eating disorders and so on. There is also the advantage of the companionship and support of others around you when making business decisions.

Partnerships

In law (including tax law), a partnership is treated as a separate entity (or person) from the individual partners it comprises. In a partnership, each of the partners is both *jointly and severally* liable for the debts of the practice. This means that each of them could be liable for all the debts the practice may incur, regardless of the proportion of the business they own, and even if they were not personally involved in the situation which gave rise to the problem or did not personally incur the debt.

Partnerships are governed by partnership law. Because they involve more than one owner, they need organisation and co-operation between the partners. Typically, a partnership agreement (preferably written) sets out the terms on which the partners have agreed to operate as a team. A partnership agreement will cover matters such as how much each partner is going to invest in the business, how any profits or losses will be divided between the partners, and what happens if one or more of them is unable to work because of sickness, death or some other crisis. I set out below the common elements of a partnership agreement. (Appendix 3: Matters to consider when entering into a working arrangement with other people).

Limited Liability Companies

A company is also a separate legal entity. A limited liability company has many of the advantages of a partnership, and one important additional one. The extent of the owners' liability (if the company goes broke) is limited to the amount of capital that has been invested by the shareholders. This is a major advantage if it is engaged in a high-risk activity such as one in which dissatisfied customers may bring legal action. A limited company will generally cost more money to set up than a partnership or sole trade, and will have additional costs such as audit and legal fees. A company is a much more formal structure than the others, and is governed by many regulations and statutes which set out rules for its operation.

Tax laws differ for partnerships, companies and sole traders, so you may need good financial advice.

So Which Structure Is Right For Your Practice?

A limited company provides the most protection in the event of becoming insolvent. A sole trade on the other hand, gives an organisation the most flexibility. When you work by yourself, you carry responsibility for everything, but also have a lot of independence. Working together with others allows you to draw from a wider range of skills and experiences, and also can provide more support, but the cost is less independence. In deciding which is best for you, weigh the advantages and disadvantages, and choose the most appropriate structure for your practice, given what you are trying to achieve. As you can see, each choice carries different implications.

While it is clear that operating a company requires you to set up the company, it is nothing like as clear for a partnership. If you are going to work with someone else under a common name the Irish Revenue or the courts may decide that a partnership exists, even if you do not intend there to be one. The test is not what you intend, but whether a person doing business with you might reasonably conclude that a partnership exists. To determine this, the Revenue or the courts might look at how you conduct your business, whether there is a bank account in the name of the business and who has signing authority, how you allocate work, pay expenses and so on.

I am greatly simplifying what is a highly complex issue, so do get legal and financial advice about what is the best structure for you before you decide.

Partnerships Or Other Arrangements For Working With Others

If you are working together with other therapists, you will probably need to create some structure to manage and organise as a group. Some useful strategies include:

- A common vision, purpose and goals
- Some form of partnership or team agreement
- Regular meetings, and
- Assignment of accountability and responsibility.

Choosing A Partner

Choosing someone to work with is a serious matter and deserves some thought before making a final decision. It's not just about being a good therapist, though of course that is important. Ideally, when you choose someone to work with, they will be bringing some additional skills that the practice needs. Perhaps you might look for management, organisational or financial skills, or some creative abilities that could be used in marketing, or a proven track record in attracting new work. At a minimum, you might check out their willingness to train or learn their way into some of these skills.

If you are going to be legally liable for debts that your partner might incur, you owe it to yourself to choose carefully. If you were going to take on an employee, you would interview them and ask for their references. You might also have a probationary period, to see if they were a good fit. Why would you do anything differently in a team or partnership of therapists?

Common Vision, Purpose And Goals

Often we can assume that others see things the way we do. When we belong to a "tribe" such as the profession of counselling and psychotherapy, we can assume that we all subscribe to the same perspectives, values and beliefs. This is not true. We each bring a unique set of perspectives, values and beliefs to the table.

In my experience, professionals coming together in a group

are carried by the excitement of the new venture and the possibility of the future. In their excitement, they can go along with things which later may appear in a different light, when conflicts and tensions arise. It is important to take the time to explore those differences, and to agree on a way in which they can be managed. These issues need to be contained in a written document. These can be detailed and formal or just include the bare bones. I set out in Appendix 3: Matters to consider when entering into a working arrangement with other people the topics that might be covered in such an agreement.

Partners' Meetings

Whether you are in a company, partnership, or group cost sharing arrangement, or other structure, you will benefit from having an organised approach to meetings that look at practice-related issues. If it's just you, consider having a meeting with another practitioner, where you can share this information. It will help to focus your activities and bring some support and accountability.

Here are some ideas to make your meetings run smoothly and effectively:

Making Your Practice Meetings Effective

- Choose a chairperson to convene and chair the meeting. This could be a position that rotates from meeting to meeting if preferred.

- Agree a time and date. A regular and relatively frequent

date (such as 7 pm on the first Friday of the month) will help to fix it in people's minds and gives some momentum to decisions and actions.

- Agree on an agenda. Many items will need to be regularly discussed and so will be on each meeting's agenda. Some will be occasional.

- Agree on the commitment to attend. Making the management of the practice a priority is an important part of taking ownership. Decisions in which you have participated will give greater buy-in.

- Appoint someone to take the minutes. Minutes can be a simple list of agreed actions and responsibilities and preferably include a time scale.

- Focus on the positives, a goal for the team is a goal for the team, no matter who scores.

But ...

- Be willing to have the difficult conversations.

- Include information about new clients (numbers, and where they came from) and any practice marketing opportunities.

- Leave an "any other business" space on the agenda which allows people to raise additional items.

What Does My Practice Need?

Elsewhere in this book, I talk about the importance of support. Support can wear different faces. It is important to have sufficient emotional support for yourself in doing this work. However, your practice also needs support. Structure and organisation can help to provide that support. A good question to ask is "If my practice had a voice, what would it ask for?" You can remind yourself to consider your practice (as distinct from either you or your clients) by having an empty chair at your practice meeting (Gestalt style) to represent the needs of the practice. I'm grateful to Ger Murphy for this useful suggestion.

Part 8:

The Fifth Pillar – Minding Your Practice

MINDING

"Trust in Allah and tie up your camel."[11]

> **Goals:** Safeguarding, security, support
>
> **Key tasks:** Identify and manage risks
>
> **Key mindset:** Willingness to create and hold boundaries

The fifth pillar of a successful practice brings a delicate sense of balance to the six-pillar structure. Where the first pillar was concerned with a willingness to take risks, the fifth pillar is concerned with managing those risks through creating appropriate boundaries. The goal of this pillar is to safeguard the practice and its most valuable asset – you.

Minding your practice is concerned with ensuring that your practice has the capacity to survive in the long term, by focusing on supporting you in your work. These supports may be concerned with your professional survival (for example, your qualification and reputation), your financial survival (by providing for your future through retirement planning), or your personal survival (through self-care).

Contracts Between Therapist And Client, Explicit And Implicit

Although the connection between survival and client contracting may not be immediately apparent, the contract between therapist and client is an important cornerstone of minding your practice. It is through the contract that we set out the boundaries of the work, and make ourselves safe.

At the outset of the therapeutic process, we talk to the client about the contract, usually in practical terms of what the work might involve, and the terms regarding attendance and fees. We discuss what the client might be looking for and how we might help with that, and we give some flavour of how we work. Thus far, the contract is explicit.

The terms of the contract are agreed between the client and the therapist. Some therapists put the contract in writing to ensure that the terms are clear. An example of a contract is included in Appendix 2: Client Contract. I'm grateful to my colleague Evelyn Burke for giving permission for this to be included.

While the terms of the contract are discussed and agreed, there is another level at which the contract may be implicit. This will vary from client to client. While this may or may not be brought into the foreground as the work develops, I find it useful to look at what I bring to the implicit contract. The following questions might help to illuminate this:

- Which of my needs do I expect to be met in this relationship?

- What do I expect from the client?

- How would I like my client to see me?

- What do I NOT want the client to see in me?

- In what way are my values and my client's values similar or different?

- What are the client's unspoken needs in this

relationship?

- What is the client seeking?
- What does the client expect of me? (And am I willing to provide that?)
- How does the client want me to see him/her?
- What does the client not want me to see?

Being aware of our own implicit expectations of our clients is useful to ground us in the work. What remains unacknowledged in the shadow has the potential to emerge in unexpected ways.

Supervision

Choosing A Supervisor

As I was training to be a therapist, and first came across the concept of supervision, I found it a rather puzzling type of arrangement. Coming from a background in the corporate world, where much lip service was paid to the supportive role of performance review and appraisal, and it was often a thinly veiled excuse for criticism and blame, I was expecting something similar. I was surprised to find that the word supervision was not a true reflection of my previous experience. Mentoring would be closer. The term "supervision" had meant for me a relationship in which a more senior practitioner manages a more junior one and takes responsibility for their work, whereas my experience of supervision in a therapy context is much more one of offering support and encouragement to one who is less experienced but whose work remains their own responsibility.

When I got over my expectation that I was being watched for the mistakes I would make and chastised for my wrongdoing, I began to relax and to look forward to supervision as a place where I could interact with another therapist about my work, for the purpose of learning and growing. I can use my supervisor as a sounding board, and receive suggestions and feedback. I am sure if I was in danger of straying into something really untoward, my supervisor would steer me in a different direction, but that is not the main focus. I suppose the greatest surprise was that the supervisors I have worked with have all trusted me to do the work I do, and this has allowed me to grow my trust in myself.

The Value Of Good Supervision

Supervision matters. It is a vital part of the network of support for therapists. In fact, a nearly or newly qualified therapist can be taken to a completely new level based largely on the support they receive in supervision. Try to think beyond the obligation to complete some supervision hours, towards your needs as a therapist, and how supervision can best support you in your work. Supervision fills a number of important roles for the practising therapist:

1. **A supervisor sees the bigger picture.** We cannot see our

own blind spots. We are too close to the detail of the relationship with the client. As I talk about my work with my supervisor, and have his experience and perspective reflected back to me, it helps me to sort what is significant from what is irrelevant.

2. **A supervisor has the wisdom of experience.** The average supervisor has experienced many more therapy sessions than the average therapist, and will have dealt with situations that novices have never seen or dreamt of. That experience is brought to the supervision.

3. **The supervisor is concerned with their relationship with the therapist, but also holds the client's best interests.** Sometimes an experience with a client triggers me and evokes a reaction which I cannot see past. The supervisor can hold both the therapist and their client, leaving space for the therapist to find something more.

4. **A supervisor can be an inspiration.** Because they care deeply about their supervisees and their development, they are able to connect with the therapist in a way that others cannot. I remember being both surprised and a little overwhelmed when a supervisor in a live supervision session at a workshop told me, "I'm here to support you." She meant it. I'd never really understood the value of support in supervision before that.

5. **A supervisor will keep you honest.** No one WANTS to

show their vulnerability, to admit they've got it wrong, or to hear that there's another interpretation of an experience with a client, but a supervisor who is supportive and kind can make it easier.

The process of supervision can reveal what is on the edge of awareness, and so help all in the triad (therapist, client and supervisor) to learn and grow. The best supervisors will get personal satisfaction in helping you be the best therapist you can be, so choose wisely.

Role Of Supervision

What do you want from your supervision?

Supervisors' styles and backgrounds vary hugely. It's a good idea to ask yourself what you are looking for a supervisor to provide. If you have recently qualified, your needs may be very different from when you have sufficient experience under your belt to apply for accreditation and different again from when you are yourself thinking of applying to become a supervisor. For example:

- What is important to you? Are you looking for technical knowledge? Are you looking for support? Is the personal relationship important to you?

- Where do they practise from, is proximity an issue?

- How do they work? Does the supervisor's training complement your own? Are they coming from a similar background as you? Do they have experience in the type of work that you do?

- Is their focus strictly on the client issues and process, or are they open to working with the therapist's process as well?

Try to get clear on your "must haves" and your "nice to haves." As with most things, it's good to have an open mind. Does your supervisor help you to stretch beyond your current boundaries? Is your supervisor open to discussing practice management issues as well as client issues? Do they discuss with you your development as a therapist, or suggest training needs?

One question that I think is particularly important about choosing a supervisor is whether you feel your supervisor can support and facilitate you when you are vulnerable and allow you to be in this place. This is essential to your ability to stretch and grow.

Therapists seek the support of a supervisor to talk about their client work. However, we cannot completely separate what's happening in the therapy room from what's happening outside. Some supervisors are willing to work with the therapist's own process. Some will also be open to working with the business aspects of running a therapy practice.

Decide what's important for you in supervision, and don't focus solely on the cost or on the requirements for accreditation. Think about where you like the balance to fall between support and challenge. Ask colleagues for their recommendations; the best referrals are generally based on personal experience. Allow yourself the space to meet a few supervisors before making your choice. It is an important relationship, and needs to be a good fit for you, both where you are right now and allowing for some growth into the future.

A colleague of mine put it well:

> *"It is important to feel that they [supervisors] are adding some significant value to your work. Particularly as a starting therapist, the work is hard enough anyway, so you need what support you can get with it. It is good that approaches emerge in supervision that would not be obvious to you. I am aware of some colleagues who would consider they stayed too long with a supervisor through feelings of loyalty. While loyalty is an admirable trait in many situations, it is not a sufficient reason to stay with a supervisor. Staying with a supervisor when the relationship is not alive does not serve either you or your clients well."*

Accreditation

Accreditation is the name given to a process whereby an organisation of therapists admit newly qualified therapists to membership, upon satisfaction of certain criteria, usually training pre and post qualification, practical experience of working with clients under supervision, together with the payment of a fee. Accreditation is generally given for a set number of years, on the expiration of which the therapist is required to renew their accreditation. The re-accreditation is again subject to the fulfilling of certain criteria, usually including completion of CPD and sufficient supervision.

Having spent years qualifying as a therapist, you may wish to become accredited to one of the bodies offering such a service. Accreditation offers the following advantages:

- Accreditation provides potential clients with a means of distinguishing between therapists. While many seekers of counselling or therapy will not be familiar with the various types and colleges of training available, and there is currently no requirement in law for counsellors or therapists to have any qualifications whatsoever, accreditation offers a means of distinguishing those who have achieved a recognised standard of qualification and experience. [12]

- Some organisations (including public service organisations) require therapists whom they might employ or to whom they might refer work to have accreditation with one of the recognised bodies.

- Membership of the accrediting body provides a therapist with a means of keeping up to date with developments in the field through courses and articles.

- The accrediting body may be a source of referrals through listing on its website or directory.

- Shortly, when qualification and registration are required by law, it is expected that accredited members of existing bodies at that time will be "grandfathered in" to the new regime, while those outside the bodies may have to undergo examinations or testing to satisfy registration requirements. [13]

- Membership of a body may help a therapist to network among peers through attendance at events, participation in committees, etc.

Accreditation cannot generally be sought immediately after qualifying. Most bodies require some years' practical post-qualification experience, together with a requisite number of client and supervision hours. Depending on the school of therapy from which you qualified, your qualification may be eligible for accreditation automatically. Some courses are approved by the accrediting bodies and others are not.

Before starting my training, I spoke to some therapists, one of whom told me that accreditation was a big issue. I was surprised therefore when I qualified to find out that the public seems to be generally unaware of accreditation. Actually, in my experience, the public are generally unaware of qualifications and training of those whose help they seek. I have *once* been asked by a client about my training. I have never been asked by a client about accreditation, other than by therapy students who are required to work with a therapist who complies with specific criteria.

The changes in the legal position will bring accreditation more clearly into focus as the line between those entitled to practice and not becomes more clearly defined.

Continuing Professional Development

One of the ways in which clients' growth is facilitated in this work is by spending time with someone who themselves is committed to their own process, growth and development. It allows clients to tap into their own drive towards self-actualisation.

Continuing Professional Development (CPD) is not just about acquiring more knowledge or learning more theory. The word development suggests something more than an academic or intellectual learning; it suggests that what is learnt is integrated and put into practice in our lives.

Each professional body will have their own requirements which you will be required to comply with as part of your membership. However, I would encourage you to see your own development as more than something you need to do to comply with your accreditation requirements.

CPD can be found in many different forms. When people think about CPD, most think about attending workshops, and these are great ways to learn, to meet other therapists and expand your network of contacts. CPD may also be gained through online training, listening to a talk by a relevant speaker, or participating in an online do-it-yourself seminar or course. Check out what's available.

Attending courses and conferences on therapy-related

matters is important, as is reading professional books, papers and journals. However, an exploration of your spirituality, learning how to keep your own books and records, or how to use a computer may also be valuable for you. You might research and write an article for a professional magazine, or give a workshop or course yourself. You might sit on a committee related to your professional body. Any activity that helps you to grow, whether recognised formally as CPD or not, helps you to expand your own range of being, and your clients will reap the benefit of your growth as much as you do.

One aspect of CPD that I encourage is to learn more about the information and skills you need in running your practice. Yes, this book is a good start, but if you are in this profession for the long haul, you really need to learn more about the mechanics of running and managing a small business. Refer to my reading list (http://tinyurl.com/je53we4) for some ideas.

Self-Care

Running your own practice can be a challenging task. Not only are you doing the client work, but there are so many other things to keep on top of.

When I worked in the accountancy profession, it was often said that "Work would be great if it weren't for the clients." It was said tongue-in-cheek but really spoke to a truth about the ambivalence that many self-employed professionals feel about the dual role of running a practice while working within it. We'd like it to be easy and stress-free, where often it's anything but!

Sometimes, of course, the client work presents challenges, especially when you're new to it. However, other challenges may also keep us awake at night, such as struggling to earn enough, keeping on top of the administrative chores, relationship issues and so on.

There are ways to make the management aspects of your practice a bit easier on you, and here are five strategies that I find useful:

1. Make A Plan!

"Alice: Would you tell me, please, which way I ought to go from here?

The Cheshire cat: That depends a good deal on where you want to get to.

Alice: I don't much care.

The Cheshire cat: Then it doesn't much matter which way you go."

(*Alice in Wonderland,* Lewis Carroll)[14]

What makes it so hard to make a plan? Is it the weight of old disappointments? Or the fear of being accountable, even to ourselves? Perhaps we're afraid we will make the wrong choice? As the cat so wisely said, if you don't care where you're going, any route will do.

If you don't know what you want, start there. Get into the habit of weighing the odds in small things. One choice will feel better, even if the difference is very slight. If you find that you look to others to decide, ask yourself what you'd like instead. Then try to take one step closer to it, perhaps by voicing your preference. An important part of owning your practice is creating an idea of what you would like it to be, and then making a plan for getting there.

2. Good Information Helps Good Decisions

Whether you're talking about buying something or deciding to work with someone, or indeed trying to make any decision, having good information is essential. Before committing yourself to anything, find out all you need to make the decision an easy one. If you don't know what you want, or what you can have, then do some research. When I decided to change supervisor a couple of years ago, I really had no idea what I was looking for so I gave myself permission to shop around. I met with three people, all of whom could have done the job well, but I listened carefully to the little voice inside which said, *"Good, but not quite what you're looking for ..."* Before making my choice a fourth option emerged, one I had not considered before, but which ultimately was the one I chose. I would never have considered that option if I hadn't given myself the space to sit with not knowing what I wanted.

3. Use Habits To Create Structure

Habits create structure and support us in our lives. They save us the effort of meeting common situations as if for the first time. Think about driving from your home to your place of work. How would it be to have to think out a route each time you took that journey? For the regular chores of running your practice, find or create a habit that works for you. For example, you could use your phone to remind you of client appointments or record your expenses in a notebook as you incur them. You could create a template for writing up your client notes or for a letter you have to write on a regular basis.

4. Find Good Support

Everyone needs support sometimes. Where would more support in your practice be of use to you? Are there aspects of running or managing your practice that could be done by someone else? Would a peer group help you to cope with isolation? Could you use some fresh ideas about bringing in clients? These are ways in which you could allow others to support you! However, many people fail to understand that the support they need most is their own support. In what ways do you deny yourself support, by judging yourself for your mistakes or your shortcomings? Perhaps you second guess yourself? Or give too much weight to other people's opinions? Could you make a habit of offering yourself more support by being kinder or more compassionate to yourself?

5. Foster Relationships With Colleagues

Therapy can be an isolated profession, especially if you work from home or have no contact with other therapists. In a very real and practical way, money comes through people. I often hear practitioners say that the only therapist they ever talk to is their supervisor!

Make a habit of getting to know other therapists and health professionals, and invest the time and effort it takes to keep in touch. The experience can be very rewarding, on many levels. A colleague shares an issue she's experiencing with a client, and you learn something from her. Someone else tells you about a workshop or a book they've attended or read, and it's perfect for you. Another colleague has a boundary issue with a client, and refers them to you instead. Fostering relationships helps to build a network that can provide support for you in ways you can't imagine.

Support And Self-Care

I apologise in advance for the clichés I'm going to use in this section, but I'm going to say it anyway:

PUT ON YOUR OWN AIR MASK BEFORE ATTENDING TO OTHERS.

This business can be demanding, particularly when you first start. If you don't consciously establish good habits, you will unconsciously establish bad ones.

Good habits are needed in the following areas to ensure your continued well-being:

- Take regular exercise.
- Eat well.
- Get enough sleep
- Have a life outside your work.

- Attend to your own emotional well-being.

- Take regular breaks.

Internal and External Support: It is important to have support in the client work. I want to talk here about two types of support, internal and external.

By internal support I mean how you feel about taking action, whether inside or outside the session, from a place of support within yourself, a place where the action is supported by your desire and ability to take it.

Think of an action you might want to take in your work, for example, something you might want to say to a client. Imagine the action is like an arm on a large machine, stretching out from you towards the other person. The arm needs to be supported by a strong, solid weight, firmly attached to the ground in order not to topple the whole structure when it stretches out. In practical terms, this means that you don't force yourself to do or say things that don't feel comfortable for you, or for which you don't feel ready. Find a way to feel more comfortable about whatever it is before taking the action. Sit with it for a while. Be curious about why it's hard for you, and what it would be like if it were easy. Let it settle for a bit.

Then there is the external support. Supervision will form part of this, and it can usefully be supplemented by peer support, either with colleagues in your place of work or with colleagues outside. This can be done in such a way as to preserve appropriate boundaries. External support helps you to grow your internal support. When a colleague or supervisor is not available, you can imagine yourself talking to them, and what they might say, and how you think and feel about that.

I believe it is a good idea to have some regular contact with other therapists. If this does not arise organically from where you choose to work, you may have to put it into place for yourself. For several years after I qualified, the group that I trained with had a regular meeting open to any of the group to come as they wished or felt able. It was a forum to discuss issues that were troubling us, or just for general support. Other places to meet therapists include CPD courses, committees attached to the governing bodies, or groups that have come together for a particular purpose, such as therapists in a local area.

Work-Life Balance: The work we do is important, it can be transformational, and it can be fascinating. It can also be frustrating, boring, disappointing, depressing and at times downright unpleasant.

IT IS NOT YOUR LIFE

I learned the hard way in a former occupation that it does not pay to invest too much of our identity in the role we undertake. We existed before this work, and God willing we will exist after it too. I have friends who are therapists, and also friends who have no interest in therapy at all. It is nourishing to have deep intimate contact with people in your life. It is also healthy to get out and have a laugh and some fun. Listening to people's problems all the time can lead us to a picture of the world as being full of problems. We may begin to believe that problems are the norm, and happiness is not real or achievable. Someone who is happy and enjoying life may be closely scrutinised for denial or repression. Every thought, word and action can be analysed for hidden meanings. There is life out there and a good one. It's short, so don't miss out.

Having other interests means that when things don't go so well in the work, as invariably there will be such times, you have other things to support and nourish you. Many therapists enjoy physical activities, such as hill walking, cycling or running; creative activities, such as art, music or writing; or other hobbies such as cooking, gardening, sewing or motorsports.

Doing Your Own Work: In my view, this is probably the most important aspect of self-care. We are all impacted by the work; some clients may impact more than others, and we need to find ways of managing that impact. I'm not saying that we should all be in therapy all the time. However, you will need to have some space and support to process what happens for you in the work.

There may be times when you may want to go back into therapy to address issues that are arising for you. I have a personal belief that this should not be an ongoing thing. In my view, the aim of therapy is to help the client arrive at a stage where they are able to manage their lives themselves in a more satisfactory way, and this applies equally where the client is ourselves. However, the other side of that coin is that we are arguably more able to help others when we have moved to a place in ourselves where our energy is relatively clear of our own issues. Many of us were drawn to the work as a means of healing ourselves. We have no idea how much we have repressed, and circumstances or events may show us a part of ourselves that needs attention. Don't ignore it.

Develop An Attitude To The Work That Supports You: I find it helpful to have a philosophy about the work that supports me. For me, this means understanding my place in the relationship with the client, my responsibility, what I'm willing to contribute, and what I'd like to get from it. It means finding a way of seeing the work that supports me as well as the client, so that what emerges in the work may help me to learn and grow, without my needs taking precedence over those of my client. I am there to serve the client, perhaps to be used by the client to heal something, but I am always responsible for my own well-being. In practice, this means there are times when I may have to put my own needs ahead of my clients' needs, by saying no, or disengaging from the work.

Balanced Portfolio Of Clients: A balanced portfolio includes clients presenting with different issues, and at different stages of the work.

Even if you specialise in one area, try to have a mix of issues that clients are presenting. It is very tough on the therapist, for example, to work mostly with clients who are depressed or suicidal, or who are very anxious.

It is difficult when you are first starting out to have a mixture of issues and stages of the work, but over time, this will develop. It is good to have a balance between clients starting, finishing and in the middle of the work. Those who are beginning their own journeys offer the excitement of what the work with them might bring. Clients winding down will hopefully offer the satisfaction of seeing some rewards as they integrate the work that has been done. Other clients offer issues that have been opened but not yet resolved, and for these the end of their journey with you may seem a long way away.

Broadening Your Client Base: It is useful to think about ways you might use your counselling or psychotherapy training in the coming years, other than in one-on-one sessions with clients. You might, for example, provide training for others in an area that you feel you have some expertise in. You might qualify as a supervisor and work with other therapists. You might use the knowledge and experience you have from a former career, and find a blend of the two. I have worked in accounting, regulation, human resources and training, as well as writing. I enjoy thinking up new ways of using these skills to expand my work and practice.

For example, I am aware of a therapist who worked in marketing before he came into this work, and in addition to his work as a therapist, he offers his marketing expertise to other therapists. Another practitioner works in IT in addition to his work as a therapist, and he offers his web design and development expertise to therapists.

Other ways of using your skills might be to work in any area in which the understanding of people might be an advantage. I am aware of therapists that work in social work, in sports, in human resources, in recruitment, in mediation, in law and in accounting. I am sure there are many other areas too.

Holidays And Breaks: When I started my practice I can remember being afraid to take holidays in case my clients discovered they could do without me and didn't come back. Eventually, I worked out that that might happen, but that I couldn't go the whole of my working life without taking a break! It is really important to allow rest, for the batteries to recharge, and to avoid burn out. Some clients may indeed decide that they can do without you, but maybe they would have decided that anyway. More clients will come.

There may be times at which you may need to pull back from the work for other reasons. If personal issues or circumstances intrude on your ability to be present for a client, you may need to take some time off. This should be decided in consultation with your supervisor to ensure a smooth transition insofar as that is possible. Having an alternate (see In Case Of Emergency … below) who can provide some cover for you in the short term is a help.

Retirement Planning

Many people look forward to when they will retire from their work and have time to pursue other interests such as travel, new hobbies, or going back to college. If this is something you've thought about, have you given any thought to how you are going to pay for it? If you're still under forty you may not have given this issue much attention. Don't leave it too long, or you may find yourself at retirement age with lots of ideas, lots of time, but too little money to put your plans into place.

At the time of writing, depending on your work history, the state basic old age pension is a maximum of between €219 (non-contributory) and €230 per week (contributory). So, if you are relying on this alone to meet all your needs in your old age, you may need to think again.

Therapy and counselling practices are *income generating* rather than *capital accumulating* mechanisms. In other words, your practice will only generate money as long as you are at work in it. And while there may be some residual value, in most cases there will be none or very little, so you should not depend on selling your practice to fund any part of your retirement.

The time to provide for your retirement is while you are at the height of your earning power, and the sooner you get started, the better. The earlier you start, the smaller the proportion of your income you will need to set aside, and, conversely, the later you start, the more you will need to save.

If you don't have an occupational pension from a previous

employment, and have not made any private provision for your retirement, it would be advisable to talk to a financial advisor or your bank about what your options might be.

In Case Of Emergency ...

If you had to withdraw from your work suddenly, through illness or incapacity, who would step in to advise your clients and find them alternative support if necessary? Would your family and colleagues know what to do?

By preparing for such an eventuality, you can make the transition easier for all involved. This issue is particularly important for those who practice on their own with no partners or colleagues.

Here are some processes you could put in place:

Contact Details

If something were to happen to you, there are people who might need to know. These should include clients (first name), your supervisor, and the name of another practitioner who is willing to see your clients on a short-term emergency basis. Include a phone number for each person. Give the list in a sealed envelope to a family member or colleague. You'll need to update it regularly.

Alternates (Also known as Professional Executors)

An alternate or professional executor is another therapist who has agreed to provide emergency holding for your clients, should you have to drop out of your practice at short notice. They may also be willing to be available for working on an ongoing basis with longer-term clients, should you be no longer able to do so. While this applies in the event of a sudden illness or incapacity, if you work with clients who are in crisis, it might also be prudent to put some arrangements in place when you go abroad or take extended leave. (You may remember how the volcano ash cloud grounded thousands of travellers, leaving them stranded abroad.) The time to put these arrangements in place is now, not when the emergency has already happened. You can read more about what should be in an alternate agreement on my website at http://tinyurl.com/hx8zddm

Therapy can be a solitary business, and in many cases, you won't have the luxury of administrative or secretarial support. If you are unable to see your clients, through a sudden illness, or family crisis, it makes sense to have an arrangement in advance with another therapist, who can contact your clients for you, and who will provide stand-in emergency cover if necessary. This arrangement takes a little time to set up and maintain but has some distinct advantages. Firstly, it helps to support clients, some of whom may be at sensitive places in their therapeutic work, and may find the sudden withdrawal of their therapist difficult to deal with. Being contacted by someone who is also capable of providing them with interim support, if necessary, gives clients a holding from which they can draw on their own resources. Secondly, from the practitioner's point of view, it can help to preserve the client relationship and, therefore, the client base for when the therapist returns to work in the future. In the absence of such contact, clients very quickly move on to finding some other way of having their needs met. In these circumstances, the financial value that you may have built up in your practice will quickly be lost.

The time to arrange an alternate is not when the crisis occurs, but in advance, so that the arrangements can fall easily into place when needed. Some practitioners advise their clients that they have an alternate and that they will be contacted in the event of a problem. Some practitioners will only advise their clients if there is a greater probability of the alternate coming into the picture, for example, if they are travelling or if there is a situation, such as family illness, which makes the practitioner's absence likely. And some don't mention it at all. It's really a question of what you think is best for you and your clients.

Personal Affairs Checklist

Most people have a personal filing system that is known only to them, and incomprehensible to even their nearest and dearest! If you weren't there to guide them, would your spouse, partner or children know where to find your will, bank statements, insurance policies or other legal documents? Luckily, you don't need to change what you do or where you keep things, Chartered Accountants Ireland has a free checklist to help you to record the location of the most common items that might be needed to be found. You can find it here https://www.charteredaccountants.ie/Global/personal affairs checklist Jan 10.pdf or http://tinyurl.com/ja4q9f8

Will

Have you made a will? Many people in Ireland grew up with the belief that making a will was tempting fate. However, if you have ideas about how you'd like your estate to be left, you should get it down on paper. Don't skimp on costs by doing it yourself, it's a small cost to have it done professionally, and you can rest easy in the knowledge that your wishes will be observed. If you don't make a will, your assets will be distributed according to law. If you would like to know more about wills and the law, Read the Law Society Guide at https://www.lawsociety.ie/Documents/pdfs/will.pdf or http://tinyurl.com/zuhma6k Or ask your solicitor or local citizens information office for details.

It might seem daunting, but there's lots of help out there. So take the issues one at a time, and by this time next year, you'll be surprised by how much you will have achieved.

Part 9:

The Sixth Pillar – Valuing Your Practice

VALUING

*You will be as much value to others
as you have been to yourself.*[15]

Bearing in mind all I've said above about the limitations that the nature of our work presents, those who wish to use their therapy practice to fund the ordinary things of life, such as buying a house or raising a family, face a significant challenge.

Are We Really That Different?

However, perhaps we overstate the situation.

While the dilemmas outlined above are real and present challenges for us, don't all professions and occupations have challenges that make them unique, and limit the scope of their activities, and the potential growth of their earnings? Some of the issues outlined above challenge other professions. For example, doctors, nurses, social workers, emergency staff, and even criminal lawyers face the challenge of vicarious trauma. Doctors face very stringent rules about promoting their services. Lawyers and accountants have detailed guidance governing their acceptance of clients, charging and receiving of fees.

I wonder at times whether we are inclined to argue for those limitations that are peculiar to our profession. Are we perhaps inclined to see them as walls that fence us in, or obstacles that we need to struggle with? Is it possible instead to find a way to engage with the challenge of growing our practices in a way that embraces our differences and sees them as gifts?

Worthiness And Deserving

We can probably all relate to issues of worthiness and deserving. We frequently have no issue in asserting the worthiness and deserving of those we work with, and yet still we find it hard to manage these issues for ourselves. They manifest directly in the discomfort that may arise from setting fees, charging for cancellations and the challenge of turning away those who cannot afford to pay. And they also manifest indirectly in the resistance we feel as we set out to market our practices.

We each have a different way of managing these issues. Some deny the importance of money completely. Some enforce their boundaries in a rigid and inflexible way. And more of us just muddle along, making choices according to how strongly we feel at the time. Each of these is a valid option, and my intention here is not to assert or reject the validity of any approach. However, I would like you to think about the obstacles that we can create to our practices being both professionally and financially rewarding.

Like most things, how we manage these issues is very much shaped by our experiences as we grew up. These experiences may have been directly related to money, but not necessarily so. We are also shaped by our attachments and our traumas. Our early experiences shaped our beliefs and values, and these, in turn, influence our decisions about money, often so subtly that we are unaware of how we make decisions about whether and what action to take. Even though most therapists are aware of how the unconscious impacts our actions, in my experience, few have explored the issue of money and financial reward in any depth.

In one of the workshops I run, we do an exercise that helps participants connect to their underlying values and beliefs about money. There is always surprise when they realise how their family patterns about money, wealth, lack, etc. are still featuring strongly in their current decision making. Indeed, even though I have been looking at these issues in myself for years, I am still surprised to find aspects of my early shaping playing out in my own practice.

The goal of the sixth pillar of a therapy practice is to flourish, to create a practice that is rewarding and satisfying. It asks us to see the value of what we offer, not just in what the client may receive from our relationship, but in what we also receive, and to allow that to be reflected in our financial reward. The sixth pillar asks us to engage with the nitty-gritty of money, to plan and put into action those steps that can support our financial health. To achieve the goal of financial reward and satisfaction, in whatever shape that might be for us, we must be open to receiving money, and see ourselves as valuable, worthy and deserving.

The Practicalities Of Money

Unless you are lucky enough to have an alternative source of income, and can afford not to be concerned with the practicalities of earning a living, you are going to have to look at money in the context of your work at some stage.

Practising therapy costs money. Whether you practice from your home or from a shared centre or a room dedicated to you, there are certain costs that will always be incurred. At the very least you need to earn enough income to cover these costs. Otherwise, your practice will be costing you money. Most people do not want to operate on that basis, either because they cannot afford to do so for financial reasons, or because, in the long term, it can lead to negative feelings, such as resentment, building up.

In the long term, I personally believe a fee should always change hands because working for nothing raises questions about the value you place on the service you are offering. Also, the client may learn about their own worthiness and deserving from you modelling for them that you place a value on your time, skill and experience. Money can also be important in marking the boundary of the relationship between you and the client.

The Cost Of Practising

The costs of running a practice include supervision, CPD, costs of providing and fitting out the therapy room (for example rent, light and heat, furnishing and cleaning) professional indemnity and public liability insurance, professional subscriptions, and promotional costs, including the cost of producing and maintaining a website. You may also incur motor or travel expenses, or the cost of eating in restaurants if you work some distance from your home.

Budgeting And Cash Flow

A budget is a way of estimating what your income and expenditure are going to be over a future period, generally a year. A budget can be prepared in two main ways, by looking at income, expenditure and profit, or by looking at cash flows in and out. If you work mainly on a cash basis (i.e., clients pay you in cash, and you pay your expenses as soon as they become due), then there will be little difference between these two methods.

However, if you work on a credit basis, for example, for an Employee Assistance Programme which pays for the work some time after it has been completed, then your income and your cash flow will be different. Why is this important? Because between the time when you do the work and when you get paid, you have to find some way of balancing your finances. You can't go into Tesco and buy your groceries on the basis that you are owed money. You need cash. A cash flow statement (or cash flow budget) will help you to identify when you are likely to need more cash, and when you are likely to have some to spare. This allows you to manage your finances in a way that will even out those fluctuations. As I said above, you can then put some money aside in times of plenty to support you when times are lean.

There is an example of a simple budget statement in Appendix 4: Example of Budget for a Small Counselling or Therapy Practice.

Setting a Fee Level

Break-Even Point

It is useful to estimate what your own costs will be, so you will know how much you need to earn to break even (the point at which your income equals your costs). Let's say for the purposes of illustration that these costs amount to €5,000 a year. You've decided you're going to charge €50 an hour. You will need to work, and be paid for, two sessions every week for the whole year to pay for these costs.

€5,000 equals 100 hours at €50 an hour.

To do 100 hours would take 2 hours every week for a year.

That's before there's anything left for your own day-to-day expenses of living (eating, clothes, running your home, etc.)

Therapy work can be seasonal, with many therapists earning less during the holiday periods. Clients are absent for any number of reasons (when they're winding down, or when they are sick, on holidays, or just doing something else.) So you can see that you really will need to have more than two clients per week to give you the income you are aiming for. Later in this section, I give a more detailed example of how to calculate what you should charge to cover your own costs.

How Much Will I Charge?

When starting out, this can be a difficult question to answer. The simple answer is that you get to decide. You are free to charge whatever you like. You are not bound by the rates your colleagues or competitors are charging, but you might find it helpful to know.

In deciding where to start you might consider the following points:

1. You don't have to charge the same fee to every client. Many therapists offer a sliding scale depending on their client's circumstances.

2. In your local area, not all therapists will charge the same amount; there will be a range of charges. In general, if your fee is within the local range, you will find it easier to be paid what you ask than if you are outside that range.

3. The terms on which the fee is charged can make a big difference to your overall income. For example, do you intend to charge for cancellations? If so, what is your policy? Here are some of the policies generally in use: Some therapists charge only for sessions attended, with no charge for cancellations within an agreed notice period. Some charge the full rate for cancelled or missed sessions. Some charge a lower rate for a cancelled session than for a session attended. Some therapists operate on the basis

that the fee is payable for a set number of weeks of the year, whether the client comes or not, the only weeks not to attract a charge being those where the therapist is on leave. This latter system has the benefit of safeguarding your income but requires confidence and courage to negotiate.

4. The client is making a commitment that may last several months or even years. The fee you initially negotiate, whether you increase it over time or not, will form the basis of the fee structure for the duration of your work. If you start too low, you may find in time that it is not adequate. You can, of course, raise your fee during the work, but you will find it difficult to raise it substantially. If you aim too high, the client may not be able to sustain it over a long term or be put off before they start.

5. A client's financial situation is not your responsibility. Their situation may change during your work. You may wish to be flexible, particularly in the short term, to enable the work to continue. Or you may not. How you respond to a request to alter the fee due to a change in the client's financial circumstances is totally up to you.

6. Don't assume that you know what the client thinks and feels about your fee. Clients vary, and so do their circumstances and attitudes, so while the cost will be a major factor for some, it will not be an issue at all for others. Some clients will make the decision about whether

to start therapy with you based on what you charge. Others will not. There are clients for whom €10 a week is too much, and there are clients willing to pay €100 or more. Where the client is in that range may not only reflect their financial circumstances but may also be affected by their values and beliefs. You get to choose who you want to work with, and so do they!

7. Bear in mind that a small variation in the fee can make a big difference to your income. If you do 500 client hours in a year (10 a week), a €1 per session increase will give you an additional €500 income in the year. A €5 increase will give you €2,500 more.

8. If you struggle with holding firm to your fee rate, consider this idea. Every time you give a discount, it is like putting your hand in your pocket and giving the client that amount of money, and continuing to give it in each and every session. Before agreeing to a reduction, check if you are okay with doing that. Your answer may not be the same for each client.

9. The level of the fee you charge will be affected by your own beliefs about what is appropriate and possible, what you believe you have to offer and what that's worth. It is useful to spend some time exploring these issues. Some of the limiting beliefs I have explored for myself since I started in practice include:

- I can't charge more than ... (my supervisor, peers,

etc.)

- Taking money for this work is wrong when people are in so much pain.

- No one's going to pay me that much, I'm just listening, not really *doing* anything.

- If I charge too much, they'll make me responsible for the outcome, and I have no control over that.

- No one can afford or will be willing to pay full price for therapy, especially if it goes on for a long time.

10. Consider how you intend to increase your fees over time. If you are planning to be in this business for a long time, you are unlikely to keep charging the same amount forever. Some therapists continue to charge the client the same fee throughout the duration of their relationship. Some increase their fee automatically each year, or every other year. Some increase the fee for new clients starting from a particular date but leave others at the rate they started on. To some extent, your decision will be informed by the basis on which you set your fee.

11. Some therapists believe the fee reflects years of experience and additional training completed or services offered. Some believe it should be set according to the area in which they live – generally country practices expect to charge less than city ones.

12. It's worth remembering too that our compensation or reward for the work comes from more than the money that changes hands. You may choose to accept less than you could because of the growth and learning that comes with the work with that client, or because you are trying to grow a reputation in relation to a certain issue. Or you might strongly feel that your worth is expressed by what you receive for your time. Transformation is priceless, and so is witnessing it.

Ultimately, you decide what to charge, so the choice is yours, and it doesn't have to be one you stick with forever.

Income Set Points

It is useful to know your own set point about arriving at a fee level. A set point is the fee level above which you personally feel uncomfortable. Most of us have set points about spending and receiving. We will find evidence to support our set points, to prevent ourselves from moving out of our comfort zones. We unconsciously filter out any options that are outside our own set points or sabotage any attempts to bring ourselves above that level. Knowing our own set points and the fears and concerns that lie behind them can help us to move past them. At the end of this chapter, I include an exercise to help you identify your own set points.

Should There Always Be A Charge?

I said earlier that I believe that a fee should always change hands. Others will disagree with me. Without being too dogmatic about it, my thinking is this: My work is aimed towards helping the clients to live their lives more effectively. In giving my services for nothing, am I perhaps looking at the other person and saying, "*I am giving you this because you can't afford to pay. I am more able than you*"? I don't believe that I do clients any favours by seeing them as being incapable in some way.

Some people will always need a high level of support to function in the world. Are they ideal clients for you? Of course, our work needs to acknowledge their frailties and struggles, and it also needs to acknowledge their strengths and abilities. Both are important.

In my view, we need to support clients towards supporting themselves. Charging a fee for the work gives clients an opportunity to take responsibility, and to contribute (however small the financial component might be) towards their own recovery, rather than expecting others to "give" the help because they are needy or wanting it.

This is a complicated issue, and I can't hope to do justice to it here. However, if this raises some issues for you, and if you haven't already read Neville Symington's piece about "Poor Mary" [16] on the subject of fees, this might be a good time to read it. You might also be interested in an article I wrote on the blog about the issues it raises for me.

http://thisbusinessoftherapy.com/kibera/

Do You Know How Much You *Need* To Charge?

So, having considered the issues raised above, do you now know how much you need to charge?

Using the process outlined earlier, we can calculate the minimum rate that we should charge to break even.

For example, you want to earn €500 a week for yourself, your expenses are €100 per week, and you work 46 weeks in the year. You might work it out like this:

I want this much income each week		500
My costs each week are		100
Total I need to earn each week		600
52 weeks in the year	say	30,000 for the year

If I take six weeks' holidays during the year, I need to bring in €650 for each week I'm working (€30,000 divided by 46 weeks). How many hours are you going to work each week?

If you are willing to work 25 client hours each week, you can charge anything from €26 upwards for each of those hours to meet your target of €650 a week. If you are willing to work only 10 client hours per week, you will need to charge at least €65 for each of those hours to meet your target.

Fee Negotiations: What's Your Style?

How do you manage the question of fee negotiations?

- You have a price and you stick to it, regardless

- You have a range of prices, and you offer what you think the client can pay

- You have a range of prices, and you let the client decide what they can afford

- You have an upper and a lower limit; you start by offering the highest, and end up somewhere in the middle

- You have a price but at the first sign of pressure from the client, you collapse and end up working for less than that, or perhaps nothing at all

There are no right ways to do this, only personal preferences, but it's worth looking at your options. Let's look at each of those styles again.

You have a price, and you stick to it regardless. The advantage of this strategy is its simplicity. You always work for your full fee, and clients can either take it or leave it. The disadvantage is that you have to be very firm to hold the line. This may be easy with someone you have never met before, but far more difficult with someone you have been working with for a while, who can no longer pay because of losing a job, or falling on hard times. It also requires you having more certainty about there being plenty of clients who can afford to pay you.

You have a range of prices, and you offer what you think the client can pay. This is more complicated than the last one and doesn't have the same certainty or clarity of outturn to it. It has the advantage of more flexibility for the therapist, who can work for clients who have a range of incomes, but for the client, the result is the same, as they are presented with one price. Offering what you think the client can pay is an inexact science, as you really will have no idea what the client can afford, or, more relevantly, what they're willing to pay, until you ask.

You have a range of prices, and you let the client decide what they can afford. The therapist declares to the client what the fee range is, and the client decides what to pay. This has the advantage of the client buying into the fee structure more readily when they have had some input into the figure. For some, it is an important part of their commitment to the process that they have had an impact on the therapist, albeit about the money. It makes the dynamic between therapist and client less one of *powerful and powerless*, and more equal. It may also be interesting to explore with the client what made them choose the point they chose.

You have an upper and a lower limit; you start by offering the highest, and end up somewhere in the middle. Again in this style, the therapist is showing flexibility, and offers her highest price, but knowing that she is willing to be bargained down to her lower one. It is for the client to ask for a lower price if the first offered is not affordable, or acceptable. If you are someone who is easily swayed by a client's sorry story, this is a good one, as it allows you to offer a discount in response, but only as far as your own bottom line.

You have a price but at the first sign of pressure from the client, you collapse and end up working for less than that or perhaps nothing at all. I said there are no right or wrong ways to do this, but looking at the practice as a business, this is the worst for the therapist, as a client's needs will always take precedence over the therapist's. If this is you, think about ways of limiting your exposure:

- Have a bottom line, the lowest fee you will accept, as in the previous example.

- Have the number of a low-cost or free service handy, to ease the guilt of saying "No".

- Limit the number of clients you take on a reduced cost basis, or

- Offer the client a reduced rate for a fixed number of sessions only.

Bear in mind that while you may be talking about the fee, you are probably not really talking about the fee. In other words, something other than money may be under negotiation here, such as an unspoken question by the client:

- Are you strong enough for me?

- Can you be flexible with me?

- Can I move you with my story?

- Do I really want to do this with you?

Since we have no idea what question the client may be asking, we have no idea what answer they may consciously or unconsciously be looking for. Clients differ, and what satisfies one will most probably not satisfy others. Trying to work out in advance how to give the right answer to satisfy the client is a mug's game, and better off avoided.

The therapist may also be using the fee negotiation as a means of setting out their stall or establishing boundaries and dynamics. For some, flexibility is a sign of weakness, and not appropriate for a therapist to show under any circumstances. For others, it may be a cornerstone of their humanity, something that is important to the client in the work.

Decide how you want to manage your fee negotiations by what works best for you, and what fits for you. Your clients will agree or they won't, but at least you will have the satisfaction of stating your own terms.

Clients May Not See Our Fees As We See Them

Don't assume you know how the client sees the fees you charge. How do we know what value others place on things or experiences? We might think they have come and continue to attend our sessions for a particular reason, but their motivation may be very different indeed. They may be interested in their own long-term development as a person, or they may want to sort out an immediate problem. They may want someone to listen to them and acknowledge them. They may want to be attended to, and heard in a deep and meaningful way. They may on the face of it be looking for a solution to a problem, but underneath looking for something else entirely, such as a relationship where they can feel safe.

When we think about the fees we are charging clients, what assumptions are we making about our clients? If we think the fee is expensive or have doubts about our worthiness or deserving, then we may assume the client will think it expensive too. They may, or they may not. If we are finding it hard to get clients that can afford to pay, we may assume there are no clients that can afford to pay. That may be so, or it may not. We may assume that a client will leave if we don't reduce our fees as they ask, and the client may well leave, or they may not.

We do not and cannot know.

Often we settle for what we think is possible. However, what we think is possible is coloured by many things, including our family of origin paradigms around money. For example, if you grew up in a family where there was a belief that "We're poor, but we're honest and good people," you may believe that to be financially secure you have to be dishonest or bad. At an unconscious level, you may then resist taking any steps that might improve your income, as to do so will bring you into conflict with your family values.

If this is resonating with you in any way, or you find the money aspects of running your practice difficult to manage, you might like to do some more reading on the subject. The following articles on my blog may be of interest to you:

- Value for Money
  http://thisbusinessoftherapy.com/value-for-money/

- Money, Money, Money
  http://thisbusinessoftherapy.com/money-money-money/

- The Place of Money in Therapy
  http://thisbusinessoftherapy.com/the-place-of-money-in-therapy/

Or you might like to attend one of my workshops on the subject. Check my website thisbusinessoftherapy.com for details.

One Last Word On The Subject Of Fees

If you feel the subject of fees is not relevant for you, if you feel called, for example, to work with those who are less well off, or who can't afford any fee, then you may need to find an alternative source of income to support yourself. In this case, since you may be giving much of your time for free or a low fee, this source of income will have to be largely passive. In other words, you need to find a way of making money that is not time intensive. Or, you need to find a source of funding, perhaps from the public purse or from a benevolent donor. This is not the subject of this book, which assumes that you wish to earn a living from your practice.

A passive source of income is one which requires little time input from you after the initial set-up stages. Examples of passive income are rental or investment income, or sales of products.

Investing In Your Practice

It can take three years or more to get any new practice off the ground, and even then, some struggle forever to earn sufficient income to support themselves. Often the response to that is to "tighten the belt" or trim expenses to the minimum to make ends meet. However, there is another option.

You could invest more money into your practice to give it the boost it needs. There are many ways that investing capital into your practice could help to make it more profitable.

In The Early Stages:

Investing some capital when you're first starting up could help you to

- Cover your expenses until your income starts to flow
- Give the launch of your practice a real boost from the start, with a co-ordinated suite of promotional materials
- Get professional help and advice to do the initial promotion

- Decorate your room in a style that suits you

- Purchase fittings or furnishings to make the rooms more comfortable

- Develop a professional website, likely to generate business

- Purchase or lease premises, which you could then sublet to other therapists

- Provide you with additional training, perhaps in business or management skills.

As Your Practice Matures:

As your practice matures, or after you've been practising for a while, an injection of capital could help you to

- Move to a better premises

- Revamp or refresh your existing premises

- Take some additional training to move you into a new arena

- Get some external advice about the best way forward for your practice

- Employ some additional help in your practice, perhaps to relieve you of some tasks and leave you free to spend time on growing your business

- Take part in a business networking arrangement.

Some examples that I have seen where therapists have used

an investment in their practice to good advantage are:

- Adapting their home to create a workspace by building on a room at the back of their home, or adding another entrance and toilet facilities. (An investment made now that will save rental costs and travel time later.)

- Investing in the training and infrastructure to start providing services online. (An investment made now to expand the geographical scope for potential clients from local to national or even global in the future.)

- Investing time (and forgoing income) in writing a textbook. (An investment made now that will raise the profile of the individual and establish them as an expert in their field in the future.)

- Investing in a second location, complementary to their main base. (An investment made now that will expand the geographical reach of their practice.)

- Investing in additional training to specialise in a particular niche. (An investment made now that will provide an expanded scope of services to offer to clients in the future.)

- Investing in creating a better website, with better search engine optimisation, and ongoing technical support. (An investment made now to create a greater public profile and broader reach, to bring in more work in the future.)

- Investing in a leasehold interest of suitable premises

which is then sublet to other therapists renting on an hourly or block basis. (An investment made now that will provide a passive income in the future, together with a bigger practice size and profile.)

Don't assume that the best way of dealing with inadequate income is to cut your costs to match. It might be, but you could also upscale what you're doing, by investing some money or time now, to make things better in the future.

Where Do I Get the Money to Invest in my Practice?

If you don't have cash lying around, for example, in savings, then a capital injection into your practice generally means one of two things: borrowing from a family member, bank or credit union, or sourcing some sort of grant aid, or both.

If you are borrowing from a family member, make the arrangement semi-formal by drawing up a contract that covers the terms of the loan. You'll need to include details of the duration of the loan, how it will be repaid, and any interest that is to be charged.

The major banks all have loans specially designed for small businesses. Check with them all to see which might suit you best. You will probably need the help of an accountant to prepare the necessary documents which the bank will need, such as forecasts of cash flows and budgets.

Local government is usually the best place to look for grant aid for establishing a small business. Check with your local citizen's information office or website.

Contingencies, Seasonality And The Need For Budgeting

As I write this, I'm looking out the window at a glorious summer's afternoon. But from a financial perspective, a fine summer is not the good news it might be. When the sun comes out, clients can often feel better. Going on holidays relieves some of the stress they feel at work or at home. Schedules start to fall away as schools and colleges close. And while it's both healthy and pleasant for us to have a break as well, the enjoyment may be tempered if you haven't made provision for the resulting drop in your income.

The regularity of work in a therapy practice can be uncertain. This is especially true when you first set up your practice.

Clearly, this can affect the regularity of your income. Unlike working for someone who pays you a salary at the end of each week or month, you may not know from week to week what your income will be. To some extent this uncertainty can be offset by your contracting with clients, and in time, as your practice matures, the pattern will probably become more regular. There will always be times when there are dips in your income, for example, when you take your own holidays or when clients who have children take a break from the work during school holidays, and there can often be a fall off during the summer and around Christmas time. Clients may come and go with little warning. There can also be times when through illness or family issues you are unable to work. If you take time off from work to attend a course, you have the double whammy of the cost of the course, plus the income you are forgoing while not seeing your clients. Perhaps this is why a lot of CPD courses run on Saturdays!

This aspect of therapy practice needs some careful managing. As a self-employed practitioner, no one pays you holiday or sick pay, so unless you have another source of income or a partner who supports you financially, it makes sense to have some system for dealing with these ebbs and flows.

There is insurance you can buy to cover your income in the event of, say, long-term illness, but most of these don't pay out until you've been sick for some months. So there will be a period when you have to cover the gap yourself.

One simple way to deal with this issue is to put a small amount of income aside into a contingency fund, which you can then draw on in times of lower income. I would suggest that the balance in this fund at any time should be the equivalent of at least one month's income. If you plan to draw on it during your own holidays, it should be more than that. One month's grace is not a lot, that's why I say it should be at least that much, but it will be enough to tide you over in the short term until you make other arrangements. In Appendix 5: Example of Setting Aside Money For Holidays I set out a simple formula for working out how much you need to set aside to cover the periods of holidays, etc.

Other choices include:

- Arranging your expenses so that they largely fall due or are paid when you have more income.

- Borrowing to cover the holiday or slow period, and paying it back when you have more income.

- Arranging your affairs with clients to achieve a constant income flow. For example, you could agree with your clients that only a limited number of unpaid holiday weeks can be taken.

With a little bit of financial planning, you can make the holiday season or slack period as comfortable as the rest of the year. And if it's a fine summer, you can enjoy the sunshine in the knowledge that your bills will be paid.

Exercise: Sticking Point

This chapter has largely been concerned with the practical issues of money. However, as I said at the top of the chapter, our ability to create a financially healthy practice requires a mindset of being open to receive, and seeing ourselves as worthy and deserving.

If you found this chapter difficult to read or to implement, you may have some underlying emotional issues regarding financial health. Most of us have them to some degree or another.

The following exercise helps to put us in touch with the unconscious that may be getting in our way.

Identifying And Exploring Our Income Sticking Point

1. Take a large piece of paper.

2. At the top of the page, write down the rate you are thinking of charging your clients.

3. Down the left-hand side of the page, write the amount of your fee if it were increased by 10%, then 25%, 33%, 50%, doubled and trebled.

4. On the right-hand side of the page, note your thoughts and feelings as you imagine yourself charging that increased amount.

5. If you find it hard to engage with this exercise, imagine yourself telling a client, a colleague, your supervisor, a former tutor, or friends and family about your increased fee level and see what comes up.

You will quickly notice a point at which the amount becomes very uncomfortable for you.

Use the following points to help you explore your fears or concerns about the consequences of earning more:

- Fears about how I see myself, or how other people see me include …

- Fears about what I might become include …

- Fears about what it might mean in my relationships

include …

- Fears about what might happen include …

There are no right and wrong answers in this exercise, so please do not use it as a reason to criticise or judge yourself in any way.

Conclusion

Starting any venture evokes mixed feelings. As therapists, we are probably more alert to them than many others. The difference between those who do things and those who don't is not that those who do things don't feel the anxieties, but that they don't let their fears drive their actions. I'm not suggesting that you act recklessly and without consideration for your own limits, but don't let your anxieties deter you from taking the first steps of what has been for many a hugely rewarding and enlarging experience. This is not a time for endless analysis of the source and history of your concerns, it is a time to focus on your desired outcome, and to see the end result of your flourishing practice, with you, happy and fulfilled, at the helm.

I hope that this short book has given you some food for thought, and will help you as you start your journey towards being a therapist. I appreciate that you may have very different thoughts from those I've presented here, and you may also have questions. I'm always happy to receive feedback, positive or negative. My views are flexible and I'm open to hearing another perspective. I'd be happy to hear from you.

Please contact me on jude.fay@thisbusinessoftherapy.com. You can also connect with me on Facebook at facebook.com/ThisBusinessOfTherapy/, or follow me on Twitter: @judefay.

Thanks for reading! If you enjoyed this book or found it useful I'd be very grateful if you'd post a short review on Amazon. Your support really does make a difference and I read all the reviews personally so I can get your feedback and make this book even better.

Thanks again for your support! I appreciate your interest. I wish you every success in your therapy practice.

Jude Fay

Acknowledgements

I want to acknowledge some of the people who have helped to make this book a reality. They say it takes a village to rear a child. Well, it also takes a village to write and publish a book.

To those who read the early drafts, and gave me feedback, thank you for your honesty and your constructive commentary. You helped me to create a better book, and I am hugely grateful for it. You include Catherine Galasso Turgeon, Padraig Timmons, Monica Haughey and, of course, my husband and friend, Peter.

To Roisin Ni Bhriain, who has consistently nudged me towards writing and publishing this book, for your unwavering faith in the value of this project. Without your belief, it would never have become a reality.

To Wei Sim Ho, for introducing me to the idea that this material had a value, by asking me to speak on the subject.

To all those who read my articles and posts, who ask questions and give comments, and to those who attend my workshops or consult me for help and support, you prompt me to ideas and new thoughts and provide the raw material from which I draw.

To my good friends and fellow therapists, Jennifer Foran and Evelyn Burke, for the support and encouragement you give me every day.

To Ger Murphy, not only for writing the preface to the book but for acting as a sounding board on so many occasions.

To those who helped to get the completed project put to bed, my editor, Emma Sherry (capitalletters.ie) and designer and illustrator Eoin Butler (behance.net/Eoin Butler).

And finally, there have been many who contributed to this book indirectly, your experience in something completely unrelated has been a catalyst to what I write, and I'm grateful to you all.

About The Author

Jude Fay is a practising counsellor and psychotherapist, living and working in Co Kildare, Ireland.

In addition to her private practice work, Jude works with therapists in developing and managing their practices. Before training as a psychotherapist, Jude worked in and for the Accountancy profession for thirty years. Her roles included private practice, consultancy, human resources and training. She brings these experiences to the aid of therapists seeking to start or develop their private practices.

Jude's philosophy is that helping clients does not need to be inconsistent with earning a living.

For some time now, Jude has been providing information and support to therapists through articles on her website www.thisbusinessoftherapy.com, a regular e-newsletter, workshops and in one to one work. Her work spans both the practical business aspects of therapy practice and the emotional and psychological issues that get in the way of creating a financially viable practice.

You can contact Jude at jude.fay@thisbusinessoftherapy.com.

Appendices

Appendix 1: Example Letter to Local Doctors

Dear Dr...,

I have commenced a psychotherapy practice at ... and write to introduce myself and advise you of the services I provide.

I will be providing counselling and psychotherapy for clients presenting with a broad range of issues including ... I use an approach which is ..., exploring feelings and thoughts, helping clients to find insight into their symptoms, and supporting them with decisions in a non-directive way.

I have a particular interest in...

I hold an [educational details] and am accredited by...

I would welcome an opportunity to talk to you, and will call shortly to arrange an appointment.

Yours sincerely,

Appendix 2: Client Contract

Client Name:

Commencing:

Confidentiality:

Sessions are confidential, with the following exceptions:

1   If the therapist believes there to be a danger of the client causing harm to themselves or another

2.   If the client reveals that there is a child at risk of abuse or a child has been the victim of abuse

3.   If the client reveals criminal activity.

Should someone need to be informed this will be discussed with you first.

Frequency:

Weekly unless otherwise agreed

Duration:

Sessions last x minutes from the scheduled starting time.

Fee:

€x per session, payable at the time of appointment. This is reviewed periodically. One month's notice will be given of any intended change.

Cancellation Policy:

If you are unable to attend at the appointment day or time, or wish to change your appointment, please give x (hours or days) notice. Your session time is reserved for you each week, therefore, missed or cancelled sessions (outside of holidays) must be paid for unless an alternative mutually suitable time can be found in the same week.

Termination:

At least one session should be allowed to discuss intention of finishing.

Medical Liaison:

The client gives permission for the therapist to consult where appropriate with their GP or psychiatrist for the purpose of discussion of their treatment or psychological condition.

Therapist Signature:

Client Signature:

Date:

GP / Psychiatrist Name and Address:

Appendix 3: Matters To Consider When Entering Into A Working Arrangement With Other People

Consider the following issues:

1. **Nature of the arrangement**: Is this a partnership, a cost-sharing arrangement or other arrangement (name it)?

2. **Who are the people involved?**

3. **Date of the agreement**: When does the arrangement start?

4. **Duration:** Is it for a fixed period of time or is it open-ended? If it is fixed, for how long? If open-ended, in what circumstances can the arrangement be brought to an end?

5. **Expectations:** Are there expectations about how much time or involvement each of you will have in the practice? (Think about outside interests, unpaid leave, holidays ...)

6. **Annual Accounts:** What are the arrangements for preparation and presentation of financial information? For example, what is to be prepared, and when. Who is responsible for preparing it? How can it be revised? Who is responsible for approving it?

7. **How are you going to divide profits and losses?** Equally or in different proportions?

8. **Conduct of practice**: Do all of the people involved have

the power to bind the others, and in what circumstances? Are some acts reserved for approval by everyone (such as borrowing money, signing leases, taking on staff)?

9. **Introduction of new people:** How does this happen? Who decides?

10. **Decision making:** How do decisions get made? Does everyone have equal rights? How do disputes get resolved?

11. **Illness or death:** What happens in the event of serious illness or death of one of the people involved?

12. **Retirement:** What happens when someone wants to retire?

13. **Insurance:** Are there requirements for holding personal insurance, PII, health insurance, etc.

14. **Pension:** Is this the responsibility of the individual?

15. **Taxation:** Is the arrangement going to have any tax implications?

16. **Salaries and Expenses**: Are salaries to be paid? How will expenses be handled?

17. **Goodwill**: Who owns the name of the practice? How is the practice to be valued when someone joins, retires or leaves? Are there any restrictions about competing if one person leaves?

Appendix 4: Example of Budget for a Small Counselling or Therapy Practice

Budget for Small Counselling Practice

Year Ended 31 December 2016

Income	**26,400**

(10 hours per week, 44 weeks, €60 per hour)

Expenditure

Supervision (26 sessions, €75)	1,950
Rent (€300 per mth)	3,600
CPD	1,500
Motor	1,500
Insurance	150
Phone	240
Subscriptions	300
Bank Charges	50
Stationery / Computer	150

Total Expenses	**9,440**

Excess of Income over Expenses	**16,960**

Appendix 5: Setting Aside Money For Holiday Periods

For this example, let's say you work for ten months of the year, and you want to set aside some money to cover you for the two months you are on holiday or taking leave. Let's say you estimate your total income (after expenses) for the year to be €12,000 per annum or €1,200 for every month you work. (10 months x €1,200 = €12,000).

To work out how much of your income you need to set aside to cover you for the two months you are on leave, divide the total income for ten months by twelve to give you available funds for each month: €12,000 ÷ 12 months = €1,000 to spend each month. That leaves you with €200 each month to put aside into a fund to cover you for the time you don't work. Once the system is established, you should have sufficient funds set aside to ensure you have a regular income all year round, even in the times you don't work.

You can substitute your own figures for my example figures in the following method:

If it's easier for you to work it out using weeks rather than months, you can use the same method of calculating simply by substituting weeks for months.

Number of months I will be working		(FIG A)	(10 above)
Estimated net income for the whole year	€	(FIG B)	(€12,000 above)
Net income earned each month	€	(FIG C) (B÷A)	(€1,200 above)
Divide total income by months in a full year	€	(FIG D) (B÷12)	(€1,000 above)
Amount I need to set aside each month	€	(C–D)	(€200 above)

Of course, in practice, it never quite works out as neatly as this, but by putting a process such as this in place you will greatly minimise the impact holiday and leave periods on your income.

Notes

[1] Hill, Napoleon (2004). *Think and Grow Rich.* United Kingdom, Random House.

[2] Millar, John G (2004). *QBQ! The Question Behind the Question: Practicing Personal Accountability at Work and in Life.* Denver: TarcherPerigee

[3] Irish Association for Counselling & Psychotherapy, Members Survey Report 2013

[4] See, for example: Gerber, Michael E. The E-Myth: Why Most Small Businesses Don't Work and What to Do About It 1990, Harper Business

[5] Attributed to Aristotle

[6] John C. Maxwell

[7] EFT / Tapping is a favourite tool of mine. If you're new to tapping and interested in learning more, please refer to the instructions on my website, http://thisbusinessoftherapy.com/eft-resources/.

[8] Storr, Anthony, 1981: *The Art of Psychotherapy.* London. Secker & Warburg / Heinmann

[9] Eddie Macken is an Irish equestrian show jumper.

[10] Attributed to Lao Tzu

[11] Arab Proverb

[12] This situation is set to change as statutory regulation of the profession is likely to be implemented imminently. However, at the time of writing this is still the situation.

[13] These changes are already underway, and are reflected in recent changes in the rules of some bodies regarding particular aspects of training. When statutory regulation of Counselling and Psychotherapy is finalised, it will mean that those who wish to practice, and to use the titles of Counsellor and/or Psychotherapist will have to register with the regulator, Coru. Registration will require them to meet the criteria set out by Coru.

[14] Carroll, Lewis (1993): *Alice's Adventures in Wonderland.* United States: Dover Publications

[15] Attributed to Marcus Tullius Cicero

[16] Symington, Neville (2007): *Becoming a Person Through Psychoanalysis.* London: Karnac Books

Printed in Great Britain
by Amazon

22486599R00149